108 WAYS TO LIVE YOUR BEST LIFE

108 WAYS TO LIVE YOUR BEST LIFE

Tiny Habits for Big Changes

SHOBA NARAYAN

HarperCollins *Publishers* India

First published in India by HarperCollins *Publishers* 2025
HarperCollins *Publishers* India, Cyber City,
Building 10-A, Gurugram, Haryana – 122002, India
www.harpercollins.co.in

2 4 6 8 10 9 7 5 3 1

P-ISBN: 978-93-6989-928-9
E-ISBN: 978-93-6989-787-2

Typeset in 11/13.7 Adobe Garamond Pro
by HarperCollins *Publishers* India Pvt. Ltd

Printed and bound at
Replika Press Pvt. Ltd.

FSC www.fsc.org
MIX
Paper | Supporting responsible forestry
FSC™ C016779

This book is produced from independently certified FSC® paper to ensure responsible forest management.

HarperCollins *Publishers*, Macken House, 39/40 Mayor Street Upper,
Dublin 1, D01 C9W8, Ireland

To

Noor, Dhruv, Kavita and Manish
for living a life dedicated to friends, family and community,
and especially books

Contents

Introduction: How to Read this Book 1

Why 108? 5

1. Core During Your Commute 7
2. Retrain Your Body While in Queues 9
3. Arise, Awake and Pandiculate 14
4. Expend Effort Effortlessly 17
5. Squat … On the Pot 19
6. Fidget 22
7. Find Fire and Water in Your Fingers 24
8. Use a Thali Approach to Exercise 27
9. Work with Your Genetic Predisposition 29
10. Game Your Time on Your Phone 31
11. Lunge in the Elevator 33
12. Suck It In 35
13. Comb Your Hair When Angry 37
14. Use Your Non-Dominant Hand 39
15. Look Sideways like a Bharatanatyam Dancer 42
16. Stop with Two Spoons … If You Can 45

17. Try to Do Contralateral Movements 47
18. Drink Water like Indians Do 49
19. Stand like an Eagle 51
20. Release Your Core Muscles 52
21. Do One Thing to Help Your Diet 55
22. Work on Your Vagus Nerve 58
23. Try Oil-Pulling 60
24. Close Your Eyes When You Walk Inside 63
25. Seed Yourself with Fenugreek 65
26. Lie on a Couch to Generate Ideas 68
27. Stare at the Horizon When You Walk 71
28. Bless the Giver 72
29. Wear Banana Shoes 74
30. Touch the Earth 76
31. Wobble While You Work 78
32. Dictate into Your Phone 80
33. Walk like a Tribal 81
34. Gain Willpower without Moving an Inch 83
35. Use the Dual-n-Back App 86
36. Know Thyself 89
37. Learn to Juggle 91
38. Become Friends with Local Herbs 93
39. Use Self Control—the App, That Is 95
40. Quantify Yourself 97
41. Track Your Habits 100

42. Figure Out How You Walk and Work 102
43. Use Synchronicity for Creativity 105
44. Drink like the Chinese and Sweat into Your Suit 107
45. Use Your Pinky for Your Smartphone 109
46. Become Aware of First Principles from the Kitchen 110
47. Watch Birds and Animals 112
48. Wear Herbal Clothes 115
49. Cultivate Tiny Habits 117
50. Sing 119
51. Overlearn 121
52. Cultivate Open Attention 123
53. Make Castor Oil Your Friend 125
54. Discover the Pleasures of Denial 127
55. Find a New Way to Look at Traffic Jams 129
56. Observe the Pain 131
57. Turn Your Enemy into a Friend 134
58. Fall 136
59. Cultivate Your Intuition 138
60. Wear Anklets 140
61. Make Friends with Your Pineal Gland 142
62. Fail Well 146
63. Avoid the Fatigue That Comes from 'Task-Switching' 147
64. Organize Your Time 150
65. Drop Lists, Choose Pleasure 153
66. Get into the Zone 156

67. Figure Out Your Shoulds 158

68. Use Lessons from the Church, Mosque or Temple 159

69. Look Up—Literally—and Look Inside 161

70. Try Other Systems 163

71. That 10 p.m. Snack 166

72. Look at a Childhood Photo Album before a Snack 169

73. Don't Phub Your Spouse, Practise the Pomodoro Instead 170

74. Work Easy Instead of Working Hard 173

75. Smell Stuff 175

76. Do What AI Cannot: Write Poetry 178

77. Oil Yourself and, If You Like, Your Spouse and Kids as Well 181

78. Keep a Journal 184

79. What's Your Poison? 186

80. Engage in Forest Bathing (Even in a City!) 188

81. Sat-Chit-Ananda: Follow Your Bliss but Find It First 190

82. Use the Alexander Technique 192

83. Frame Your World with the Right Words 194

84. Keep Your Mouth Shut 196

85. Don't Use Maps 198

86. Surrender to the Muse 200

87. Pen Down Your Dreams 203

88. Marry Your Cellphone 204

89. Be a Gardener Instead of a Carpenter 207

90. Hug Trees 209

91. Roar like a Lion 211

92. Talk to Elders 212

93. Read Poetry and May Your Tribe Increase 215

94. Look at an Empty Space or Eternity 218

95. Describe Wine in Five Words or More 219

96. Use Your Cell Phone for Divination 222

97. Why Balance Wins 225

98. What Verbal Personality Type Are You? 229

99. Doodle 232

100. Embrace Dualism 233

101. Gargle and Swirl after Eating 236

102. Be Vulnerable 237

103. Consider a Smidgeon of Fear 240

104. Play Ancient Board Games 241

105. Call Your Mother 244

106. Don't Be Deaf to Your Body 247

107. Walk, Don't Drive, to Buy Fruits 250

108. Eat like Our Elders Did 253

Acknowledgements 255

Notes 257

The detailed notes pertaining to this book are available on the HarperCollins website. Scan this QR code to access the same.

Introduction
How to Read this Book

I WAS BORN TO write this book because it is how I live my life. As a restless person, often characterized as a 'Vata' type in Ayurveda (restless, prone to movement), I have a stack of tools that I use to get fit. I alternate through them and adapt them to the situation. I've tried every single practice in this book. I'd like to think I've invented some of them, too. This book is nominally divided into categories: physical, mental, emotional and practical. The physical includes methods of working your body: the cognitive, with the mind and memory; the emotional, with the self and relationships; and the practical, which includes products and apps that can help you in your efforts. That being said, the whole point of this effort is to embrace a holistic life.

So flip a page or two, choose a practice to try out for size, adapt it to your life and off we go.

There are many chapters on the same topic, smartphones being one of them. Like a prism, they shine the light on different aspects of this giant behemoth that rules our lives. I haven't touched upon AI and ChatGPT much because their effects are still being felt and have yet to be studied.

Some of the chapters offer contradictory advice, which is a function of who I am and how I think. I test out hypotheses till I find them to be true. Then, I move on to another, possibly opposite hypothesis to test it out. I end up taking elements from both. A friend derides me as the least consistent person he knows, which is another way of complimenting my contradictions. You see what I mean about holding two opposite thoughts in your head at the same time? What he thinks of as an insult, I capture as both an insult and a compliment: something we Indians are adept at doing. Then again, who was it that said consistency is the hobgoblin of small minds? I looked it up. It was Ralph Waldo Emerson in his essay titled 'Self-Reliance',[1] published in 1841. The whole essay is a paean to independent thinking and exhorts you to trust yourself, trust your thoughts, and walk your own path. In it, Emerson says,

> A foolish consistency is the hobgoblin of little minds, adored by little statesmen and philosophers and divines. With consistency a great soul has simply nothing to do. He may as well concern himself with his shadow on the wall. Speak what you think now in hard words, and tomorrow speak what tomorrow thinks in hard words again, though it contradict everything you said today.—'Ah, so you shall be sure to be misunderstood.'—Is it so bad, then, to be misunderstood? Pythagoras was misunderstood, and Socrates, and Jesus, and Luther, and Copernicus, and Galileo, and Newton, and every pure and wise spirit that ever took flesh. To be great is to be misunderstood.

Well, let every parent whose kids have misunderstood them take heart from this essay.

There are many chapters on alternative techniques and therapies. Use them as you will. Depending on proclivity, with scepticism, or full-hearted acceptance.

There is also an unhealthy amount of references to bhujia sev, mostly because it is my snack of choice. Also, because much of this book was written while munching it.

Two accusations can be levelled against this book: that it is a leap of faith or a leap towards folly. Depending on your worldview, you can use either or both.

This book isn't rocket science. It doesn't aspire to be. It attempts to rock your science, though, through a simple set of suggestions. Some are common sense; some are based on science; some will make you roll your eyes (and doing that is a good exercise, by the way, so go ahead and do it); some will make you snarl with exasperation—and again, if you are doing that, you might as well go all out and do the Simhasana or lion's pose.

Some suggestions are weird enough that they could only come from one person's mind: mine.

So, feel free to leave this book at a place where you do your quick reading, be it in the bathroom or next to your bed. Open a page, read and follow. That's it.

This book's 'physical' section operates on one principle: continuous exercise. By that, I don't mean exercising all the time—while you eat, drink or sleep—although creative readers of this book will find ways to do that. It means exercise every time you think about it. If this sounds like a lot of work, it actually isn't. The tips I suggest involve taking sensible shortcuts, maximizing wasted time and choosing exercises that give maximum benefits.

Some of you already go to the gym and have regular training routines. This book is not for you. This book is for people like me: people who like variety.

The mental part of this book has to do with acquiring a flexible, facile mind. A lot of this has to do with creativity and generating ideas. Some are very good at it, while others plod along, working hard, making lists and sleeping on it. Some of us have trouble remembering these lists, and there are suggestions for that too.

As numerous apps and books point out, we can use small nudges and techniques to push ourselves further towards our goals, keep laziness and sloth at bay, and fast-forward the steps we take. This book contains an incomplete list of products and techniques I have tried.

At the end of some chapters, I have included an Indian proverb. India is a land of poetry, metaphors, proverbs and myths—all rich in earthy and imaginative imagery. This is how Indians speak; for us, it is a way to remember messages. It took time and effort to find the right proverbs, and I hope you enjoy each one.

Read on. More importantly, do.

Why 108?

FOR HINDUS, BUDDHISTS AND Jains, 108 is a sacred number.[1] Mathematics calls it an abundant number, tetranacci number, refactorable number, Achilles number, Harshad number, semi-perfect number, and self-number—all great qualities to have. The term 'Harshad number'[2] was coined by Indian mathematician D.R. Kaprekar (who has Kaprekar's constant named after him). The meaning of 'Harsh' is joy. There is a beautiful Sanskrit word for hair standing on edge. In Sanskrit, they call it 'romaharsh' or happy hair ('roma' meaning 'hair' or 'bristles' in Sanskrit).

According to the 2012 book, *The Four Foundations of Mindfulness in Plain English* by Bhante Henepola Gunaratna, in Theravada Buddhism, 108 comes from a nifty addition that is linked to the senses.[3] Take the five senses, then multiply them by the three feelings (pain, pleasure and neutral), and then multiply them by whether they are externally or internally generated and then to time (past, present or future), i.e., 5 x 3 x 2 x 3 = 108. Only a Buddhist can take apart emotions in such a structured and precise fashion. When you feel bad the next time, introspect about these aspects.

The Nepalese parliament has 108 seats. In Buddhism, there are 108 self-realized saints. Although very different from Hinduism, the Jewish faith has a certain mysticism associated with the numbers 1 and 8. Jews traditionally give gifts in multiples of the number 18; you could argue that 108 has enfolded these two numbers. Jainism, too, views 108 as a sacred number.

In Hinduism, 108 is linked to both Shiva and Vishnu. The number of Shiva's ganas (warriors) is 108. Vishnu as Krishna, danced with 108 gopis. In the Srivaishnava order, there are 108 Divya Desams or divine realms of the Lord.

The way I remember it, though, is astrologically. Vedic astrology has twenty-seven 'nakshatras' (Sanskritic lunar mansions). Each has four 'paadas,' or legs or sections, and 27 x 4 = 108. The number 108 permeates Hinduism. There are 108 poses in the south Indian classical dance form, Bharatanatyam. Indian martial arts believe that there are 108 pressure points in the body. Hinduism also links 108 to the cosmos; the distance between the Earth and the sun is 108 times the sun's diameter. Similarly, the distance between the Earth and the moon is about 108 times the moon's diameter.

Sun's diameter = 13,80,000 km

Distance between the sun and the Earth = 14,96,00,000 km

14,96,00,000 ÷ 13,80,000 = 108.4058 (which is rounded off to 108)

The 2016 paper, 'The Attractiveness and Significance of Numerical Number 108,'[4] says that 108 is the number that Kundalini ascribes to 'energy lines' in the body, and 108 are the ways in which this internal energy communicates with God. I mean, if 108 is how we speak with God, no wonder it suffuses sacred architecture and literature.108 is the number of the cosmos, nature, sacred rites and the chapters in this book; it is also the first word in the title *108 Ways to Live Your Best Life*.

Hence, 108.

1

Core During Your Commute

WHEN I'M STUCK IN traffic, my usual modus operandi is this: I slump back in my seat and curse fluently. One day, I tried something different. Since I was feeling bloated, I decided to sit upright by moving a couple of inches forward on the seat instead of slumping back as usual. My bloating didn't go away, but there was a side benefit. I discovered that I had to engage my core muscles to sit upright as the car zigzagged its way through traffic. I have been doing this ever since, not continuously but sporadically, when I think about it, which, by the way, applies to every chapter in this book. It's not as if I follow my suggestions all the time. I do these things some of the time, and so should you. But back to core during your commute.

Caveat: This is only possible when someone else is driving and if you have no previous spinal or joint problems (hip, knee, ankle). Consider it only if you are a passenger, not a cab, bus, train, tram or subway driver. I do this exercise, or should I say, non-exercise, while I drive, but I have a few years more than you in terms of trying this out.

Engaging your core while in the car is simple. All you need to do is sit upright. Make sure that your back doesn't lean against the backrest. No matter what happens or how much the vehicle jerks or turns, don't lean back. That's it. If possible, pretend that there is a rod going through your spine. Hold that position for the length of the ride. You will be surprised at how tight your abs feel at the end of the trip.

Staying upright isn't a simple task. It took our ancestors millions of years to figure out how to go from ape to Neanderthal to Homo erectus to Homo sapiens. Sitting upright in a wildly swerving car, bus or autorickshaw hardly simulates this magnificent evolution, but at least it is better than reclining. If you are able to get driven around, tell your cab driver that you are in a hurry because this exercise works better if you have a maverick driver who brakes hard and then accelerates the car abruptly. After a forty-five-minute car ride, with you sitting in this position, you are ready for the advanced level.

This, too, is a seemingly simple practice. Lift your feet off the floor while sitting in the car. Just lift your feet a couple of inches off the floor. That's it. Hold your position. After a while, your thighs will start hurting, and that is the purpose.

Harder than you think, isn't it? Your back has no support, so you must rely on your core to sit upright. On top of this, your feet are off the ground.

Stay for just three minutes in this position if you can. Feet up, don't lean back. Keep your hands on your lap. Your reflexes will ensure that you grab the handles if need be. At the end of the ride, notice how tight your abdominal muscles are.

Sitting upright has another benefit: it improves your willpower.

As social psychologist Roy Baumeister says in his book, *Willpower*, one of the first experiments his lab did had to do with posture. He says,

> The assignment was just telling people to try to work on their posture. 'Whenever you think about it, stand up straight, sit up straight.' They did that for two weeks. Then, we gave them a bunch of lab tests that had nothing to do with posture, but they showed significant improvements in willpower compared to the control group. You can really improve your capacity for self-control.

The great thing is that you can do this work while speaking on the phone. You can get your meeting done and work out your core muscles. Every commute becomes a gift.

2

Retrain Your Body While in Queues

WHAT DO YOU DO when you stand in a queue—at the airport, inside the plane after landing, at a bus stop, or in your pharmacy waiting for a prescription refill? Most of us check email, WhatsApp and social media, look around at the weirdos who have whipped out their phones the second the plane lands, judge them and enjoy the halo of self-righteousness floating above our heads. All that's done, but your turn in the airport's security queue still hasn't come. What do you do? Here's a thought: why don't you reset your brain?

There are dozens of body-mind therapies that aim to reset the damage at that time, injuries and bad habits have done to our bodies and minds. Following them for decades, I am steeped in all of them. Look up somatic therapies, and you will come up with a long list, and this doesn't even include ancient civilizational techniques such as Indian yoga or Chinese Tai chi.

There are a number of newer therapies. It would take an entire book to describe them, plus there are already books that do exactly that. So let me just leave you with a list of names with the suggestion that you look them up if they are of interest. Here is a partial list of the things I have tried or studied: Hakomi, Feldenkrais, Trager, EFT or Emotional Freedom Technique, Alexander, Havening, BCST (Biodynamic Craniosacral Therapy), Rolfing, and so on.

So, what are somatic therapies and how do they work? Let me turn to an article from *Harvard Health*[1] to explain this, and yes, I am intentionally using this bastion of higher education in order to get your buy-in. Somatic therapy is 'a treatment focusing on the body and how emotions appear within the body', as stated in the article. 'Somatic therapies posit that our body holds and expresses experiences and emotions, and traumatic events or unresolved emotional issues can become "trapped" inside.'

Each of these somatic therapies operates differently, but they all share a few things. The first is a belief that the body learns bad habits—bad ways of moving—for a variety of reasons, ranging from accidents, surgeries, repetitive tasks, multitasking, injuries, and emotional stress. The results are patterns of tightness and contracted muscles that end up in pain.

The second, as stated in the above quote, is that the body holds these patterns inside, resulting in physical and emotional symptoms, all linked to pain.

For example, let us say that you fracture your left ankle. During the road to recovery, your body compensates for the pain you feel in your left side by using the right side of your body to do more tasks. Months later, even after your left ankle has healed, your brain continues to rely on the right side. The brain, like me, is looking for maximum benefit with minimum effort. Nobel-prize-winning behavioural economist Daniel Kahneman calls this 'Cognitive ease' in his 2011 book, *Thinking, Fast and Slow.*[2] The way that the brain does this is by making many instructions automatic, for instance, lean right. All well and good; necessary for healing. Except that the brain forgets to reverse the instruction once the left leg heals. Pretty soon, your body is tilted slightly, almost microscopically, to the right. And so, it goes. A lifetime of hurts, sprains and cramps results in chronic irregularities within the body, resulting in pain as you age.

So, what's the solution? If I had to summarize the many distinct somatic therapies I have tried into one or two takeaways, it would be this. Figure out a way to move with awareness. This means that when you do routine tasks like making coffee or folding clothes, see where you hold tightness. Close your eyes and pay attention to how you move. Do you always lead with one leg? Is your breathing shallow?

Are you carrying more weight on your right than on your left? Are you tightening your jaw or shoulders where many of us hold tension? Are you leaning your head forward to create 'the computer neck', which looks like a slight bump in your neck? Many of us have this: look around.

There are two ways to process pain and hurt, physical or emotional (often, the two are interlinked). One is through talk therapy, and the other is through somatic therapy. Having studied psychology in college, I have followed both methods throughout my life. Each has its virtues, and I use them both.

Somatic therapists believe that physical and emotional pain is stored in the subcortical regions of the brain, i.e., below the prefrontal cortex, which is responsible for logical thinking. The subcortical brain is accountable for automating processes like breathing and reflexes and adjusting or adapting the body when a body part is fractured or hurt. These automatic processes of adaptation help us function. The trick to preventing chronic pain is to override this automatic subcortical instruction. Movement therapists compare it to 'clearing out the cache' of your brain so your body is returned to its original state. Somatic exercises, in that sense, are a way for the body to renew itself, to erase old instructions that are no longer relevant.

Several things are required to practise somatic exercises. The first is to prepare for the movement, which means you pause, take a breath, and do the next movement with intent. The second is to do the movement slowly, very slowly. The third is to do it without effort or pain. You don't push yourself. You don't stretch more than you need to. It has to be effortless. The fourth is to breathe while doing this. The fifth is to reverse the movement and return the body to its original position.

It doesn't matter what movement you do. If you pause, prepare, do the action effortlessly, focus on the action and return to the original position, that is good enough.

Let us think of a simple movement. You are moving your head from left to right. In a normal stretch, you tilt your head and push yourself to stretch it till the point of pain. That is not a somatic stretch. The point is not to push yourself but to pay attention to the movement. Make it easy on your body, but force the brain to focus on the action.

At this very moment, I am doing a simple somatic exercise. I am lifting my shoulders. That's it—no effort, just a lift. But I'm paying attention to my body. As I lift my shoulders gently, I can feel a slight constriction between my shoulder blades and a little pain in my right shoulder blade. Where did it come from? I don't know. Perhaps it is an old injury. Just acknowledging this pain and constraint allows our brain to reset its commands.

Another simple 'somatic reset' exercise is to do the cat pose in yoga. A group of people also recommend crawling on the floor since it is the first movement that we learn. I tried crawling, but frankly, it felt weird. What helped was to start on all fours, as if I was going to crawl and then stretch backwards and forwards.

A somatic exercise that dancers practise is rolling slowly on the floor. Like doing the 'anga-pradakshanam' at Hindu temples. Except that you do this slowly and mindfully.

I have found that a great time to do somatic exercises is when a plane has landed and people are waiting for the doors to open. Most people stand uncomfortably in line to get off the plane, as mobility in a packed aisle is not easy. You can use that time, literally a few minutes to pay attention to which part of your body feels tender or painful and then gently move or stretch it with attention.

Somatic exercises don't take too much time. They don't need too much effort. In fact, they should not be effortful—they should be effortless. The point is to do them often and with attention.

The best part is that somatic exercises feel really good. Do these often enough, and their benefits are far-reaching. Not only do you gain physical agility, but you also gain mental peace and centredness. Now that the generalized context is given let me give you a specific one.

When you are waiting at the bakery counter for your bread to be sliced or in any other queue anywhere, pull your stomach in or do butt crunches. What are butt crunches? Well, it is basically about tightening your butt. Hold for fifteen seconds. Release. Repeat.

Start with ten times and then work up to a hundred crunches per time. So long as you aren't wearing tight jeans, nobody will know. And if you are butt-crunching while wearing tight jeans, the people behind you will watch in speechless fascination.

I hope that you become like a Pavlovian dog. The minute you get into a line either at the bank or post office or at the airport, your butt crunches into a tight ball. Many actresses do this, which is why their posteriors go viral.

3

Arise, Awake and Pandiculate

IN THE LAST CHAPTER, I talked about somatic exercises. In this one, I want to go to the motherlode. The person who coined the term 'somatics' is a philosopher-turned-movement therapist called Thomas Hanna. He created a series of exercises to do the resetting that I discussed in the last chapter. His therapy rested on a simple concept: pandiculation. Studies show that the Hanna method can reduce back and neck pain, and it is all done through pandiculation.[1] I know—it sounds like a bad word. but it isn't

Think of the last time you woke up—not with an alarm, but naturally. What did you do? You probably constricted or tightened your muscles briefly before stretching—arms above your head, feet downwards. After engaging in this luxurious stretch, you probably relaxed.

Think of how your pet dog or cat wakes up after a nap: feet forward, belly down, back arched upwards, and perhaps a yawn to go with it. We think of this movement as a cat stretch, but these animals aren't stretching. They are pandiculating.

A pandiculation is a constriction of muscles followed by a stretch. Constrict, release, relax, that's the sequence. Animals do this effortlessly. There is no thought of 'pushing' themselves or taking their effort 'to the next level' to beat this week's fitness goal. It is just part of their being.

Animals pandiculate some forty times throughout the day. It is their way of relaxing their bodies. Human embryos pandiculate during gestation, and babies and children continue to do this throughout childhood. Watch how a baby wakes up; you will understand the pleasures of a nice pandiculation.

Our bodies are built for many things, but we also have the capacity to experience pleasure—not just because we are getting a massage, but because movement is intrinsic to who we are as humans. Relearning how to take pleasure in all the simple and complex movements that our bodies are capable of is a wonderful and fruitful art.

It isn't just for pleasure, though. According to a 2011 paper by Luiz Fernando Bertolucci, 'Pandiculation: nature's way of maintaining the functional integrity of the myofascial system?',[2] published in the *Journal of Bodywork Movement Therapies*, argues that 'pandiculation might preserve the integrative role of the myofascial system by:

a. developing and maintaining appropriate physiological fascial interconnections; and
b. modulating the pre-stress state of the myofascial system by regularly activating the tonic musculature.

What does this mean in plain English? The myofascial system is like a thin skin that covers our muscles. Sometimes it gets inflamed. Here is the thing, though. A muscle ache or pain you feel in one particular part may have its origins elsewhere. Just because your calves hurt doesn't mean you only stretch them. Even doctors concede that aches could come from remote parts of the body. Bertolucci's paper argues that since our entire musculature is connected, pandiculation is a way of toning the entire body and preventing chronic and local pain.

So how do you do this? Much like somatic exercises, it is about paying attention. As adults, caught up as we are in alarms and deadlines, we forget how to do a simple, luxurious stretch with intent and attention. So, the next time you get up from a chair after an hour of working on the computer, consider pandiculating. Constrict (tighten your body) and then release it into a lovely long stretch. That's it. To relearn this, pay attention to the pandiculation stretch you do when you wake up (and many of us have forgotten even doing this when we wake up because we are all reaching for our phones). Relearning pandiculation, which we did as babies, and repeating this action throughout the day will help us.

A pandiculation is not a prescribed movement. Simply shifting your head from side to side while you wait for your morning coffee is a good start. In other words, you can invent your stretches; do what makes your body happy, do what feels right. You can arch your body back or forward. You can bend sideways. No matter what movement you go for or which muscle group you choose to pandiculate, do it slowly and comfortably. That's the main thing.

Your tight muscles will thank you for it. Your old injuries will slowly heal themselves. To some degree, chronic pain in old age can be averted. Pandiculation is a somatic reset of your brain so that old injuries dissolve and don't turn into chronic, arthritic pain.

These simple constrictions and intentional but quiet stretches are not heroic or difficult. In the long term, they may be the best thing you can do for your myofascial system and, indeed, your whole body. Who knows? These small steps may even give you the strength of an elephant, not because you are lifting weights but because you are dissolving old hurts and pain.

4

Expend Effort Effortlessly

THE MOST FAMOUS VERSE in the yoga sutras of Patanjali is arguably, '*Sthiram sukham asanam*'. Sthiram means grounded, stable, motionless. Sukham means pleasant, ease-filled, beatific. Asanam refers to posture. This verse, (*Yoga Sutra* 2:46) tells us to ease into every posture we hold and figure out a way to make it stable, and pleasant.

The next verse (*Yoga Sutra* 2:47) tells us how to do this: '*Prayatna shaithilya ananta samapattibhyam.*'

Prayatna means effort.

Shaithilya means relaxation, dilation, looseness, dropping, slacking, reducing.

Anantha refers to endless, eternal joy.

Samapatti-abhyam refers to a confluence or coming together; things that merge or coalesce when you focus attention on them.

Taken together, it means that by reducing effort and focusing the mind on the infinite (or emptiness), you gain anantha or bliss in every pose. Essentially, the verse asks you to let go of harsh effort, focus on the movement and softly unite with the infinite. Stretch as if doing a yoga asana, and then relax into the pose. Sure, there will come a point of pain; when you reach it, stay there (as the yoga gurus say). Westerners call it embracing the pain, but I like our Indian instruction to 'stay there at the point of pain' better.

Founder of the Iyengar yoga method, B.K.S. Iyengar translates it as 'Perfection in an asana is achieved when the effort to perform it becomes effortless and the infinite being within is reached.'[1]

Effortless effort seems like an oxymoron, but it is key to balance. Slack off a bit, says the verse. Loosen up. Effort is necessary, but like everything else in yoga, it has to be in moderation. It has to be gradual.

This is not just gobbledygook. Try this. If you are sitting, stand. Then, perform a stretch. It doesn't matter whether you decide to stretch sideways and touch your hands to your extended leg or toes, or you bend forward or back. You will reach a point when it hurts, after which you can go no further. Hold the pose at that point and then exhale. Sigh deeply and relax. Stay there. Or, if you prefer the Western phrasing, embrace the pain. Sigh and go deeper into the pose. The goal is to attain a certain equanimity, a certain poise and later, a sense of joy in this movement that you are holding.

Which part of your body stores your tension? For many, it is the shoulders. For some, it is the back of the neck. After a couple of hours of tapping away at the computer, where do you feel the tightness? Does your back feel painful?

If so, consider this. Stand up for a second. Slowly lift your arms towards the sky. Hold your fingers together and gently allow your head to fall back. All this is done very slowly. Close your eyes, hold this pose and sway a little, breathing deeply, and feeling your shoulders loosen. The point is not to stretch too much. This isn't an exercise. This effortless effort leads to relaxation at first and unity with the infinite when you evolve. The goal is to dissolve the tightness that you feel in your shoulders. After a few breaths, you slowly release and let your hands down.

In this age, when effort equals reward, doing less doesn't feel comfortable. You feel like a fake.

'Working out' has a halo effect because you experience some pain and, later, some gain. However, in the long term, knowing the balance between effort and effortlessness is the key to growth, not just in yoga but in life.

How much effort do you put into a venture? When do you decide to stop and let go? When do you choose to 'cut bait', as they say in finance? All these are judgement calls. Perhaps the way to attain this judgement is by the everyday practice of this effortless effort. Maybe the real takeaway is just to keep moving.

5

Squat ... On the Pot

I ASKED A FEW experts for one exercise that would give the greatest value for time spent. I was hoping they would say, 'Eat chocolate, in moderate quantities, throughout the day.'

Instead, they said, 'Squat.'

I did, and so can you.

You are probably doing squats anyway because they don't require specialized equipment. They can be done anywhere: while waiting for the tea to brew, for the copy machine to warm up, or while speaking on the phone.

Think of the phone calls you get every day. Maybe your mother calls you every morning. Or your child studying at a faraway college calls. What do you do during these random everyday calls? What do you do when you are on hold? Squat, I say.

Squats use some of the most important—and biggest—muscle groups, such as the lower back, the buttocks, and the upper thigh. You can do them while watching TV, the news, or whatever it is you close the evening with.

Squats also help retard the ageing process. If you look at octogenarians, the one thing that they have difficulty with is getting up from a chair without help. Squats directly help this activity. The trick is to do it right. You keep your feet one shoulder-width apart. Fold your arms in front of you. Then, go down with your back straight. The way that you do this is by pushing out your butt or by gazing upwards.

In the beginning, you go down as much as you can without keeling over. The goal is to squat low enough that your thighs are parallel to the ground as if you are sitting on a chair that doesn't exist. Lift yourself; go down; lift yourself. That's it.

Squatting isn't new. Every coach tells you to do this. But many of us forget that squatting is something we can do anywhere. Got a minute between meetings? You can get a few squats in. Doing squats everyday strengthens these muscles and helps you lift yourself up, quite literally, in your golden years.

My earliest memory of my dad is of him squatting on the floor, surrounded by piles of paper. An English professor, my father read exam papers from students on the romantic poets he loved or researched linguistics, all by squatting on his haunches on the floor for hours. Perhaps as a result, I, too, am a squatter.

India is a nation of squatters. Drive through the countryside, and you will see men and women of all ages squatting under trees as they wait for buses or to share taxis. Indians of the previous generation can sit in this way for hours. It is the most intuitive and relaxing posture, not just for sitting but also for shitting and childbirth. It is how the human body aligned itself to rest before chairs were invented. Chairs, along with sugar and smartphones, are modern-day scourges. Sugar, you can avoid. Smartphones, less so. But squatting can be cultivated.

The bestselling book *Gut: The Inside Story of Our Body's Most Underrated Organ* by Giulia Enders[1] explains in scientific language why squatting while you go potty is good for the elimination system. The book spawned the sale of numerous 'squatty potties' in the West, marketed by a pink teddy bear excreting ice cream.

We in India have been squatting to take a shit for centuries. The Indian toilet is a great invention. It uses less water and gives you a more satisfying excretion. There is only one problem. Most Indian homes are slowly graduating to Western toilets. How, then, to squat?

Gut suggests a solution. The main thing about squatting on the potty is that your legs are elevated to the level of your stomach. Think of how you squat on Indian toilets. Now, here is what I do to simulate this. I take the wastepaper basket that is available in every restroom, no matter whether you are at home or in a hotel. Sit on your western toilet and place your legs on top of the wastepaper basket. It will take you a few trials to get into the groove, but once you manage to raise your legs off the floor (as high as possible), your gut will thank you. This will help eliminate the toxins better from your body.

The other thing to do is to build an Indian toilet into your master bathroom alongside a Western one if you have to. Like a bidet, this can hark back to our past and give you an excuse to squat. Most suburban homes have ditched the Indian toilet for the Western one. But what have we lost in the process?

6

Fidget

I DON'T FIDGET, BUT maybe I should. A new study published in August 2016 in the *American Journal of Physiology: Heart and Circulatory Physiology* showed that tapping your feet while sitting for extended periods of time reduces the risk of heart problems.

Jaume Padilla, a professor of nutrition and exercise physiology at the University of Missouri and the lead author of the study published on 4 August 2016 in *Science Daily*, 'Toe-Tapping to Better Health: Fidgeting Helps Prevent Arterial Dysfunction from Sitting,' said,

> Many of us sit for hours at a time, whether it's binge watching our favourite TV show or working at a computer. We wanted to know whether a small amount of leg fidgeting could prevent a decline in leg vascular function caused by prolonged sitting. While we expected fidgeting to increase blood flow to the lower limbs, we were quite surprised to find this would be sufficient to prevent a decline in arterial function.[1]

So, if you can't rise and walk around during your next lengthy meeting, he said, tap your toes. Bob your feet. Keep your legs in motion somehow, no matter how slight. And if your spouse or aisle mate should frown in annoyance, point out that science now says that fidgeting is good exercise.

Fidgeting is an underused exercise, as are other things we can do with our legs. No matter how much we exercise, there are times when we can do nothing; when we just have to sit and listen. Or so we think.

Allow me to break that little misconception. Think about when an unexpected guest drops in. You haven't seen Uncle Fernandes in years, and after half an hour of listening to his old army stories, you realize why you made sure not to see him in years. What are you going to do? You cannot get up and leave. You have to stay put and have a polite conversation.

Think of a classical music concert or a lecture. Think of those long meetings where you must just sit and listen to people drone on and on. All you can do is sit still and listen, right? Or maybe not.

I thought of leg exercises during a long Western classical music concert. Now, you may be one of those people who knows exactly when a symphony is supposed to soar, which year Mozart wrote his piano concertos, and what mood he was in when he wrote the fifth movement. I don't. After an hour of undivided attention to the orchestra. Well, not really. Ten minutes of undivided attention, I begin fiddling.

Leg exercises are great for when you are forced to sit in one place and not move. There are a whole bunch of these exercises.

When I am tired, I simply stretch my feet to rest on the floor under the chair in front of me. Then, I tighten my knee, which looks and feels as though I am pulling up my knee cap. I hold this position for fifteen seconds and relax the knee cap, which rolls back down. Do fifteen repetitions. It strengthens the knee joint and gives you something to do during a long classical music concert or a lecture.

Range of motion exercises with your ankle is another option. Simple ankle rotations, curling your toes in and out, or tracing the alphabet with your feet are other ways of stretching and flexing your legs.

Using your feet in the most innocuous of places—while sitting—won't feel onerous even when you are at a long pointless meeting and will benefit you long term.

7

Find Fire and Water in Your Fingers

IT IS THE END of the day. You are tired. You don't want to stretch, you don't want to squat. You just want to veg out in front of the TV. How do you optimize this experience?

An easy way is to learn some mudras. Mudras are gestures that use the fingers of the hand and are found in Buddhism and Hinduism. In India, they are described in the *Natya Shastra*, an ancient treatise of dance. These mudras operate under the principle that each finger is affiliated to one tattva or element.

Memorize this if you can: thumb for fire, forefinger for wind, middle finger for akash or ether, ring finger for earth and little finger for water. By holding the fingers in a certain way, the theory is that you can affect the movement of energy within the body.

The forefinger is the wind element, so if you feel gassy or bloated, you join the tips of the forefinger and the thumb or place the thumb on top of the forefinger. The little finger is the water element and if you feel parched or dry, you touch the little finger with your thumb to balance out the water element. Typically, you hold each mudra for fifteen or twenty minutes while sitting with your back straight.

My favourite is the surya (or sun) mudra, which is thought to reduce weight. Bend your ring finger. Place it at the bottom of the thumb. Rest your thumb lightly on top of your ring finger. Keep watching your show. Half an hour later, you would have burned some calories without moving a limb. In fact, you shouldn't move a limb while doing mudras.

Just sit, cross-legged in padmasana (lotus pose) if you can, and hold still with your mudra.

Tibetan monks use mudras to generate internal heat in freezing winters and balance their body elements throughout the year. You can do them while sitting on the train, watching TV, stuck in traffic, or while waiting for your kid to come out of basketball practice. You can do mudras in parties while pretending to listen to a lengthy discourse on stock picks from a drunk stranger.

Chinese medicine believes that the health of the body can be measured through the flexibility of our fingers. You don't need to press hard while doing mudras.

There are countless books and papers on mudras. Begin with the Hatha Yoga Pradipika, which lists out ten mudras and bandhas that destroy death.

> *Mahamudra mahabandho mahavedhascha khechari*
> *Uddiyanam mulabandhas cha bandho jalandharabhidhah*[1]
>
> Meaning: Maha Mudra, Maha Bandha, Maha Vedha, Khechari, Uddiyana, Moola Bandha and Jalandhara Bandha.
>
> *Karani viparitakhya vajroli saktichalanam*
> *Idam hi mudradasakam jaramarananasanam*[2]
>
> Meaning: Viparita Karani Mudra, Vajroli and Shakti Chalana, truly, these are the ten mudras which destroy old age and death.

A more contemporary version is Rekha Rao's 'Mudra Vijnana: The Science of Hand Gestures in the Female Figures of Rani Ki Vav,'[3] which talks about how you should use and hold mudras. The pressure of your fingers, for example, should be light and fine, and your hands should be relaxed.

You may find that you cannot do all mudras with both hands. I have trouble touching my little finger to my thumb in both hands. I have to hold it in place with one hand to use the other. This is okay to begin with and will gradually get better.

Like anything else, paying attention to how your body reacts helps improve this practice. Touch your little finger (the water finger) with your thumb and see if you start salivating or if your eyes start tearing up. Does it actually balance out the water element like they say it does?

My yoga master told me to do the shankha-mudra or conch-mudra for forty-five minutes while I watched television. It would help my hypothyroidism, he said. Sit still, hold your hands in the mudra, and breathe evenly, was all he said. Even doing this proved difficult. I tried. What happens is that you fidget after a few minutes. Suddenly, your back itches. Watching TV helps because you are so engrossed in the show you forget your hands.

Ideally, you would learn mudras from a practitioner, but since it is a gentle healing art, learning it from the many websites on the Internet wouldn't hurt. One mudra I have been experimenting with is called the Hakini mudra. It involves touching all five fingers of one hand with the corresponding fingers of the other hand. It is supposed to improve memory and concentration. As it happens, tapping both sets of fingers is a common gesture that people do when they are thinking deeply. And so, it goes with other mudras. Some of them are intuitive. We do this anyway without realizing it. In their ease, lies the beauty and healing qualities of mudras.

One thing that I am noticing as I get older is that my fingers are not as flexible as they once were. When I hold certain mudras, one finger bends, another hurts, and the third one doesn't stretch fully. Then I wonder: if our entire body is contained in our hands as the mudras would like us to believe, will working on my fingers improve the corresponding body parts? And if so, wouldn't it be cool?

8

Use a Thali Approach to Exercise

MORE AND MORE STUDIES point out the benefits of High-Intensity Interval Training (HIIT) or doing a series of exercises in short but intense bursts of 1 to 2 minutes.

Gretchen Reynolds, *The New York Times* health columnist, was one of the earliest proponents. In 2009, she wrote an article with a provocative headline, 'Can You Get Fit in Six Minutes a Week?'[1] in which she quoted studies that documented how intense exercise for a short time would help people get fitter.

Apps, such as those that provide a seven-minute workout, play to this trend. Essentially, all these results point to doing a series of activities (like a thali) in short spurts but in an intense way. The catch lies in the word 'intense'. As Reynolds says in the article, 'There's a catch, though. Those six minutes, if they're to be effective, must hurt.' It is like those karelas (bitter gourds) on your thali.

So here is a choice. Walk forty-five minutes on the treadmill, which is called MICT or Moderate Intensity Continuous Training, or race-up five to ten flights of stairs to the point where you feel breathless, like your lungs are going to explode. However, this will not work for those with heart or lung issues. Personally, I would pick the stairs because you get the benefits of exercise in a few short, if painful minutes.

The logic is that this was how our palaeolithic ancestors 'exercised'. They ran away from threats in a life-or-death spurt of speed, following which they normalized and took it easy. Animals still do this. The good news for us is that we can incorporate the principles of HIIT by figuring out a way to exercise.

For me, that is sprinting around a nearby army campus, forcing myself to maintain the highest speed that I can muster till I become breathless, till it hurts. The way I do this is to pretend that a lion is chasing me as I run. It simulates (somewhat) how our ancestors would have dealt with danger.

If you don't want to sprint outside, use a skipping-rope and jump for a few minutes quite fast. The real advantage of HIIT exercises has been documented in a 2021 study, 'Evidence-Based Effects of High-Intensity Interval Training on Exercise Capacity and Health: A Review with Historical Perspective'.[2] It says that HIIT exercises solve an important problem: the barrier to entry.

'It is well-documented that regular exercise is essential for a healthy life, but insufficient time to exercise seems to be one of the most cited barriers to exercise adherence,' says the study.

If we only need a few minutes, there is really no excuse for doing HIIT exercises.

But since this book goes beyond exercise, here is how you can incorporate HIIT into your life. Every time you are late for a meeting, and you have to run—do that. Don't just walk fast. Run. Every time the Uber driver calls and says he is downstairs, race down the stairs, taking them two at a time. After dropping your kid at the school bus-stop, run home instead of walking. These small jolts of high-intensity exercises keep you supple and nimble.

The best part is that, just like dishes on your dinner thali, you can vary the exercise components. Just as long as they make you feel the pain.

9

Work with Your Genetic Predisposition

THERE IS THIS LOVELY word in Ayurveda, 'prakruti', which alludes to your genetic predisposition. Robert Svoboda has written a 1998 book on it called *Prakruti: Your Ayurvedic Constitution,* in which he lists all the permutations and combinations that make you *you.*

Prakruti is a very particular combination of genes, circumstances, and attitudes. This is obvious anytime you observe a loved one. Each child is different even if their home environment is the same.

Prakruti has to be taken into account in your fitness regimen too. Do you have a preference for one type of exercise, maybe running or Pilates? Or do you prefer a variety of fitness exercises that you rotate through? Are you self-motivated or do you rely on a trainer? Do you exercise intensely and erratically, or do you prefer moderate exercise that is consistently done? All this depends on your prakruti. So how do you work with it?

Linking exercise to one place (the gym, yoga class, the park) has the benefit of focus and consistency. But it is also limiting, in that it lets you off the hook once you do that morning run or weightlifting. And how regular are you with your daily gym exercises anyway? Don't answer that if you are one of those disciplined, super-regular folk.

The trick for mere mortals like me is to figure out ways to keep ourselves active all the time. Shopping is a case in point. You enter a shop to buy things, right? Wrong. You go in to stay active. When you reach down to pick out the noodles or pasta from the bottom shelf, squat instead of bending. When you want to pick out stuff from the top shelf, stand on tiptoe for ten seconds, maybe fifteen. Stretch to reach for sachets of tea.

The other place to stretch is when you cross the threshold to the doors. Most of us use our hands, largely to type into our smartphones these days. We don't swing from, or even reach for the trees, as we did for millions of years. One way to correct this is to use the threshold of doors. Anytime you cross the door in your home or office, reach up to touch the top of the threshold. If you are tall enough to reach it, grasp either end, pause for a second and stretch. Your body will become concave, stretching out your upper body. If you cannot reach the top of the doorway, hold the sides of the door and similarly stretch till you experience a gentle pull, then let go.

Valerie Berg, a Rolfing teacher, talks about 'structural ageing,' in a wonderful podcast called *The Liberated Body.*[1] In it, she says that the body shrinks and contracts as it ages. One way to counteract this is to figure out ways to stretch and expand. Berg does it by placing her commonly used kitchen items—sugar, coffee, tea—on the highest shelf of the kitchen and not on the counter. This way, she has to reach up and stretch when she wants them. The idea is to create an environment, both at home and the office, where it is easy for you to move and, if possible, exercise, which, when you think about it, is the whole point of this book.

The idea is to work with your prakruti.

10

Game Your Time on Your Phone

HOW MUCH TIME DO you spend on the phone each day? A few hours? Likely, isn't it? And what do you do when you speak on the phone? If you are seated at your desk or in a cubicle, I beg you, do something while talking—at least lift some weights. If you need to type on your computer while on the phone, flex your feet or stretch them out under your table. Then draw circles with your toes. Stretch your hamstrings.

The easiest thing to do, of course, is to walk while you talk on the phone. This is something that all of us do these days, which itself is a problem. In my building's garden, I can barely talk to neighbours because everyone is on their phone while walking, except the elderly, who know the art of chit-chat and its benefits. But back to walking. If you have a one-hour conference call, get yourself some excellent headphones and walk around your office floor while on call. Climb some stairs.

I find standing on tiptoe while I talk on the phone is also great, particularly if you have connectivity issues and cannot move around too much. It doesn't take too much room, you don't need a large office to do this, you can do this pretty much anywhere.

Recently, I have found a killer exercise to do while on the phone at home. Get one of those large balance balls that you use to sit on or you use for Pilates. Do the yoga pose called 'chakrasana' on it. It is like a backbend on the ball.

Sit on the ball and bend back till your head touches the ball. You are almost in a convex, inverted C position. Then, talk on the phone in that position. Your middle will get a nice, inverted bend, your stomach muscles will get a gentle stretch, and your head will arch backward and rest, which rarely happens. The only problem is that your voice will change to the point where everyone will ask if you are inside a well or have the flu.

Caveat: you need to have some experience in yoga before taking baby steps into this pose. It is a bit disorienting at first and you need to figure out what to do if the ball rolls sideways. You don't want to lose your balance. Take slow steps.

If this ball pose is difficult or you don't have a ball, then consider lying on your bed with your head hanging from the edge. This is an easier pose, and your head will still get to arch backwards. The only problem: your friends will wonder why you don't want to hang up. And why does your voice sound so strange, almost strangled?

Another exercise I do while on the phone is to wall-sit: pretend I am sitting on a chair while using the wall for back support. My mother calls me at 7 am every day, and when I talk to her, I wall-sit. Our calls are short, often under two minutes. We talk mostly to hear each other's voices—have you had coffee, that sort of thing? So, stretching or wall-sitting is easy.

You can also use tools such as pillows, balls, chairs or whatever is at hand, to push yourself into an unusual stretch or a pose while on the phone. It is a way to exercise without the pressure of exercising.

In his book *Tiny Habits*[1] Stanford Professor B.J. Fogg uses an 'If This Then That (IFTT)' approach to exercise. My version is this: If I lift my phone, I will do some exercise. It could be anything, but as long as the phone is in my hand, I will stretch or jump or wall-sit.

Linking movement or exercise with your mobile phone is a powerful habit that forces you to incorporate pain (exercise) with the pleasure and addictiveness of reaching for the phone. It requires willpower for the first several times, but hopefully, later, it will become an unthinking habit. After all, as writer Annie Dillard famously said, 'How we spend our days is, of course, how we spend our lives.'

Please don't think I do this exercise stuff every time I pick up my phone. But I do it when I think about it. I do it occasionally. And for our purposes, that is enough.

11

Lunge in the Elevator

IN 2010, IBM SURVEYED some 6,500 office workers across multiple cities in the United States to find out how much time they spent waiting for elevators and inside elevators. It turns out that IBM's New York workers spent a total of 16.6 years waiting for elevators and 5.9 years inside elevators, when tallied over 12 months.[1] Readers of this book likely spend a ton of time in elevators, too. This is both limiting and liberating. Limiting because you cannot speak on your phone as reception is poor. Liberating for the same reason.

There are a number of things you can do in the elevator: read a book (maybe this one), say your prayers silently or check your phone, which is what most of us do anyway. These options are offered up in case you are tired of the usual things we do while stuck in an elevator—stare stonily up at the floor numbers and wait for that reassuring 'ping' sound that will allow us to escape that claustrophobic space.

Now, here's a thought, and you know what's coming, right? Why not use those few moments to get some exercise in? After all, you missed your Pilates class this morning. Since the elevator is crowded, try upper body stretches. Clasp your hands behind your back and roll your shoulders back to combat the hunch that comes from working at computers all day.

The other thing is to face the wall—away from all those sweaty bodies—and flex your feet so that your heel is on the floor and your toes are touching the wall. This gives your calves and lower legs a nice stretch. Lean forward to amp it up a notch.

If you are an entrepreneur with a start-up, you can practise your elevator pitch, thus flexing, quite literally, your muscles and your mind.

If you are alone inside, the best thing to do in an elevator is to lunge. This is particularly true if it is a small to medium-sized elevator. You know the kind where you crowd in, shuffle around like a penguin, and hope that everyone is wearing deodorant? This is exactly the size of an elevator that is perfect for lunges. The length is perfect to spread your feet forward and do, say, ten lunges. Halt only if the elevator stops in the middle and folks enter.

Then again, if you are halfway through your lunges, why bother letting go?

12

Suck It In

ASHTANGA YOGA HAS A practice called 'oddiyana bandha'. In its original and authentic form, this practice helps awaken your kundalini and, therefore, needs to be learnt from a proper guru. The asana has to do with pulling in your stomach. Trained yogis can suck in their stomach so that it goes flat below the rib cage. For the rest of us, simply doing the following practice can help. Exhale completely. Pull the stomach in as much as possible. Hold the position. Lift your diaphragm and hold.

Most of us begin by holding our breath while the stomach is pulled in, but my yoga teacher tells me to gently inhale and exhale using the top part of the respiratory canal while holding the stomach in. Do this for ten to fifteen seconds. Repeat.

Another option is ab exercises. When I first went to the gym, a fitness trainer began my session by making me lie on the ground and do 'pretend ab crunches'—pulling in the stomach without lifting my head, unlike in a normal abdominal crunch. When I first tried it the muscles in my stomach hurt the next day, which tells you how out of shape I was. But it also tells you the power of imagination. When you pretend you are doing ab crunches, your mind believes it is doing the crunch. Muscles hurt.

Such imagination can work when you want to buy things you don't need or cannot afford. Pretend you own those expensive sunglasses or handbag. Simply imagining this can prod your mind into releasing all those happy pheromones that come after a good day, a good purchase or for that matter, a good night in the bedroom.

I can do real ab crunches now, at least in theory. The question is: why bother when pretend-pulling in the stomach offers comparable benefits, at least on the happy endorphins front? Sure, I am simplifying, but the point is, what can you do when you wait at the airline gate, waiting for your flight to be called? Pretend ab-crunches, that's what. You can do these when no other option is available.

I do it in a crowded elevator. It has one added benefit. Pulling in your stomach is easier if you hold your breath. Then you don't have to smell anything in that crowded elevator. And if people look at you funny, like your face looks like a pinched monkey, just know that not everyone can appreciate everything.

13

Comb Your Hair When Angry

I WAS STANDING IN line to renew my driver's license. The line was long. The clerks behind the counter seemed to be pursuing one goal: to make each person's experience as long and as miserable as possible. People waiting their turn checked their phones and read magazines. All of us had the resigned looks of those who knew they were in for a fruitless, painful morning.

Then, along came an elderly woman, sidling past everyone, muttering incoherent apologies under her breath—something about having to leave soon and trying to barge in the front of the line.

We each have our trigger points, and mine happens to be queue jumping. Put me in any line—at the airport or in a government office—and my blood pressure goes up. I become like a wary tigress waiting for her first unsuspecting prey—crafty, inconsiderate queue-jumpers. When I see someone jumping a queue, I go white-hot in anger. The blood rushes up to my ears, almost deafening me in the process. I consider throwing things at them, like custard apples and egg yolks on their face. Mostly, I yell; which is what I did when this old woman jumped the queue.

'Oy!' I yelled, 'What on earth do you think you are doing?'

The suspect tried to slither away, but I walked up and shamed her into resuming her proper place at the back of the line, and that restored my equilibrium.

People offer many tips for anger management. They tell you to breathe deeply. They suggest that you practise loving-kindness meditation, which doesn't make sense to me. How can you feel kind, let alone loving, in such situations? These days, I am trying a new technique that stems from anger management. Every time I spot somebody doing something that enrages me, whether it is jumping the queue or extending bureaucratic red tape to the point of no return, I choose an activity that is so far removed from my current state that it distracts my mind. It could be something ridiculously simple such as searching for lipstick in my handbag, running a comb through my hair (crazy though it looks) or retying my shoelaces. My mind is forced to pay attention to something else. It works for me.

Try this when you are white-hot mad. I'm sure it can work for you, even in the case of road rage. While you may not calm down, you certainly will not explode. Those few seconds may be all that is necessary for the culprit to leave, thus depriving you of the opportunity to shame-yell them into submission.

As for the simmering anger inside, just do the Palaeolithic run as soon as you can, i.e., run while pretending that you are being chased by a tiger. It will expend all the rage and energy you have bottled up.

As for me, the next time someone causes me to seethe, I will take deep breaths and use these techniques to distract myself. I will tell myself that the irritation is just as bad like a bear enters a bedroom. The only thing to do in that situation is play dead.

14

Use Your Non-Dominant Hand

JUST LIKE OVER 90 per cent of the people in this world, I am right-handed. Actually, I am a suppressed lefty, not in the ideological but physiological sense. I was left-handed and my parents made me right-handed. Scientific and wild theories exist as to why the human race is overwhelmingly right-handed. Some say that people are right- or left-handed based on how they were positioned in the womb.[1] If the right side faced outside, it received the most stimulation, turning you into a left-handed person. That's the theory anyway. Others talk about the spear and shield used in ancient warfare. The spear was held in the right hand, which, therefore, became dominant.

Paul Broca, a nineteenth-century French neurologist, whose name happens to be one of the seventy-two names inscribed on the Eiffel Tower, discovered a speech centre in the left hemisphere of the brain that ended up being named after him as Broca's area.

Being right or left-handed and what it means has been debated through the centuries. Psychiatrist Abram Blau wrote in his book *The Master Hand*, 'We are right-handed because we are left-brained,'[2] something that French sociologist Robert Hertz upturned in his book *Death and the Right Hand* by saying, 'We are left-brained because we are right-handed.'[3] Now, this might sound like a tautology, but it is actually a deeply felt critique of the human race. Hertz, like Benjamin Franklin before him, who wrote a spirited defence of the left hand, believed that choosing one dominant hand (the right) had caused all kinds of problems for humanity.

For one thing, this ubiquitous dependence on the right hand caused humans to adopt left-brain thinking, which was more dualistic than holistic, dividing the world into good and evil, right and wrong, and black and white. Had we encouraged ambidexterity, felt Hertz, perhaps we as a species would been more intuitive, compassionate and open to our feelings, somewhat like ancient tribal societies with a higher proportion of left-handedness: Pygmies, Aborigines, Bushmen and Hottentots. The world may have been a better place without this zero-sum thinking.

In 1981, Roger Sperry won the Nobel Prize for his research on the two hemispheres of the brain. His work showed that the right brain largely controls the left side of the body and vice versa. The right hand, therefore, is connected to the left brain, which is the seat of logic, language, analysis and reasoning. The left hand is connected to the right brain, which is the source of images, creativity, insight, spontaneity and feeling. Several US Presidents by the way, including Barack Obama, are left-handed.

Today, much research on this subject is done from the point of view of sports. Does switching from the dominant hand to the other (left instead of right, and vice versa) improve a basketball player's ability to throw? An Indian research team, whose study was published in the *Indian Journal of Clinical Anatomy and Physiology*, has even studied whether vegetarian table tennis players have a softer hand grip than non-vegetarian players.[4] It concluded, by the way, that 'a well planned vegetarian diet is recommended for an athlete because of its antioxidant properties'.

For our purposes, attempting to use your non-dominant hand is a worthwhile goal. Most of us go through life unconsciously using the hand that we are comfortable with. Using our non-dominant hand, however, has fascinating repercussions, according to recent research. It improves willpower and self-control and opens up aspects of our brain that we are not in touch with.

As Lucia Capacchione describes in her book, *The Power of Your Other Hand: A Course in Channeling the Inner Wisdom of the Right Brain*,[5] simply writing or drawing with your non-dominant hand will increase imagination, childlike imagery, and open up parts of your personality that have been long suppressed. I have started doing this on my iPad, using free apps such as Paper or Sketches. It is somewhat hard to use my left hand, but it also fires different neurons and works different muscles.

What do you do when you confront the door? You reach out to open it with your dominant hand. What if you cannot? So, practise using your non-dominant hand. It could be simple things: stirring tea, opening the car door or brushing your teeth—all with your non-dominant hand.

The logic is that using the non-dominant hand forces you to use different muscle groups and may help to enhance self-control and willpower. The effort involved in using the non-dominant hand equalizes the brain hemispheres and evens out your temperament. Who knows, it may spark your creative thinking and help you forge a new path in whatever you are engaged in.

15

Look Sideways like a Bharatanatyam Dancer

INTERMEDIATE BHARATANATYAM DANCERS LEARN a technique called 'alarippu'. The technique, which you can see demonstrated on YouTube, involves moving the eyes from side to side to a specific tapping rhythm. I find it beautiful but viewed through a non-Tamilian prism, it could look weird. No other culture has dance forms that incorporate as much eye movement as the Indian classical and folk dances do. Not Japanese Kabuki and Noh dances, not Chinese folk and opera dances, and certainly not Western ballet. They use their bodies, but their eyes are still. Not so with Bharatanatyam, Kathakali or Kathak, where the eyes dance and sway to express and draw people in.

The Art of Looking Sideways, to quote the book title and philosophy of the late great graphic designer Alan Fletcher, has been perfected in India. Bharatanatyam especially includes sideways eye movements, or what brain experts call 'horizontal saccades'. A saccade is when the eyes rapidly move from a fixed point to another fixed point.

Here's the thing. Studies have consistently discovered that these horizontal saccades improve memory. The reason has to do with how our brain is wired. The right hemisphere is connected to certain aspects of the left side of the body and vice versa. So, moving your eyes left will activate your right hemisphere, which is the seat of imagination, intuition and creativity, and moving them right will activate the brain's left hemisphere, known for logical and analytical thinking. This is easily demonstrated in kids. Ask them a question and see where their eyes dart.

'How come you didn't do well on the test?' If the eyes move left, thus activating the imaginative right brain, the kid is probably inventing an excuse.

'If Aryabhatta has twenty-seven mangoes to be split among forty-five students, how many mango pieces will each person get?' And no, the answer is not 'Too few'. The eyes move right to activate the analytical part of your brain.

If your eyes saccade—you look sideways, left and right, in quick succession, it will activate both brain hemispheres and cause 'inter-hemispheric coherence'. We do this anyway during our REM (Rapid Eye Movement) sleep to consolidate our memory of what happened during the day.

A 2017 study titled 'Effects of handedness & saccadic bilateral eye movements on the specificity of past autobiographical memory & episodic future thinking,'[1] posits that these 'bilateral saccadic eye movements' help improve 'episodic memory'—the type of memory that keeps track of autobiographical information.

This is the who, what, where, when and why of our lives. Where did I keep my keys? When is my meeting? Who did I see at the party? Why am I here—not in an existential sense but more in the forgetful 'I know I opened the fridge for a reason, but I have forgotten what I want,' sense. That is a function or a failure of episodic memory.

In contrast, semantic memory broadly remembers general knowledge, ideas and facts accumulated throughout our lives. We need both types of memory, but the one that is most associated with absent-mindedness is episodic memory.

In 2013, Sander Nieuwenhuis of the University of Leiden and his colleagues had a cool spin on the connection between eye and memory. They showed, like others before them, that bilateral saccadic eye movements enhance memory retrieval. With one addition. When they tapped the left and right hands of the subjects alternatively, memory improved. But not when sounds were played in alternate ears. The study, 'Bilateral saccadic eye movements and tactile stimulation, but not auditory stimulation, enhance memory retrieval',[2] published in the February 2013 issue of *Brain and Cognition* indicates 'contralateral organization of the visuomotor and somatosensory systems'. In simple English: our senses of vision and touch are connected in an X-shaped fashion to the opposite side of the brain. Not so with hearing.

How does this help us?

The next time you are in what I call a 'rush to retrieve' mode, try going shifty-eyed. You have to run out of the door but have forgotten where you kept your cell phone, house keys or spectacles: objects without which you cannot leave. Try this, just stand still for thirty seconds and shift your eyes horizontally from side to side. Or let's say that you are a college student taking a quiz, where you have to regurgitate lots of facts. Just before you enter the exam hall, find a quiet corner and move your eyes from side to side for thirty seconds. After saccading your eyes, go in and write the exam. You will perform better.

Since reading this, I have started moving my eyes from left to right while brushing my teeth in the morning with my non-dominant left hand. I don't recall the names of every star and planet that I see in the sky, but I do recall the Latin names of the birds that surround my building: the black kites are *Milvus migrans*; the red-whiskered bulbuls are *Pycnonotus jocosus*; the house crow is *Corvus splendens*; and those infernal pigeons are *Columba livia*.

16

Stop with Two Spoons ... If You Can

'EAT LESS' IS ONE of those phrases so vague as to be almost meaningless. Everyone who knows that you are trying to lose weight trots it out—trainer, nutritionist and even the random passerby. The problem with this instruction is that it is hard to implement. Of course, I want to eat less. I just don't know how to. If I did, I would be fifteen pounds lighter.

Over time, many of us come up with a blueprint of how to eat less—whether it is using dieting apps or getting a weighing scale and counting calories religiously with every meal. All of this requires work and discipline. Here is a slightly easier approach: whenever you eat something that is highly calorific and highly tasty, stop after eating two spoons.

It is simple enough instruction, and therefore you cannot avoid it. It also forces you to savour those two spoons, because they are going to be your last for the day or meal—for that dish anyway. When you think about it, whether you're eating a rich chocolate cake or a deliciously creamy ice cream, two large spoons (or four tiny spoons) are really all that you need to savour and enjoy the dessert. After that, it is really about shovelling down the rest.

Hold on, don't just take my word for it. A study titled, 'Pleasure as a substitute for size: how multisensory imagery can make people happier with smaller food portions',[1] published in October 2016 in the *Journal of Marketing Research*, shows that when subjects were asked to vividly imagine the taste, smell and texture of a chocolate brownie, they ended up choosing and enjoying a smaller one—without any sort of overt or covert nagging or guilt-tripping. So this is another approach. When I am faced with a tres leches cake or a tiramisu, I gaze at it for some time, imagining its creamy texture and rich taste, all in the hope that this type of visualization will persuade me to eat less.

Pleasure, as the study found, is inversely related to the size of the portion. It is at its maximum in the first few bites, then goes down with every additional bite. The last bite is crucial and determines the overall impression of the dish. People who choose large portions do so for two reasons: hunger and value for money. Focusing on pleasure helps people naturally choose smaller portions.

Professors Pierre Chandon of INSEAD and Yann Cornil of the University of British Columbia tried another version.[2] They imitated the descriptions that customers get at fine dining restaurants, using terms such as 'aromas of honey and vanilla' with an 'aftertaste of blackberry'. Such vivid descriptions made 190 adult Americans—used to supersized portions—choose smaller portions, as compared to a control group where the dish was simply described as 'chocolate cake.'

Most of us eat so fast that we don't let our stomach catch up and tell us it is full. Savouring a meal by using your imagination is a way of sabotaging this process. So, the next time you are confronted with a chaat, biriyani, pizza, tiramisu or ice cream, pause for a minute. Close your eyes and imagine the taste of the dish that you are just going to eat. Imagine its crunch if it is a potato chip. Smell its aroma and visualize its texture on your mouth if it is a pizza. Then, come back to the real world, pick up a knife and cut the pizza in half. I guarantee you that you will enjoy the half portion as much as you would have enjoyed eating the whole of it.

I am not saying that I stop after eating two spoons of dessert each time. But I do pay attention to those two spoons, and occasionally, I'm able to distract myself, so I don't reach for the third, fourth or fifth spoon just to 'eat for taste' or 'nappasai' as we call it in Tamil.

The trick to stopping yourself when you don't have the willpower is to get up and leave the table. Go to the bathroom and splash some water on your face. Or walk away to check your phone. Just walk away.

17

Try to Do Contralateral Movements

YOU HAVE JUST POPPED your coffee into the microwave and set it for one minute. What do you do? Just stand and wait, right? Why not try a contralateral pose?

Contralateral movements? What's that, you ask? It is the most simple and intuitive movement where the two sides of the body are doing two opposite things. Pretty much every activity that we do naturally is contralateral: walking, running, swimming, climbing up a tree. Essentially contralateral is a fancy way to say what we say in our school March Past (right-left, right-left). Whenthe right leg moves, the left arm moves. That's it. That's contralateral movement. The way it is defined makes this simple movement appear so complex.

One definition says, 'A contralateral pattern is the opposing movement of the hips and shoulders on both sides of the body. When the right hip moves forward, the opposite arm follows and vice versa. Coordinating these opposite sides of the body requires us to pass information between what is commonly called the two hemispheres of our brains. A complicated explanation, isn't it? Just say walking.

The problem these days is that we don't swing our arms enough when we walk, thus allowing for that lovely contralateral movement. Similarly, we don't take long steps. To counter this, swing your arms while walking and try long strides. And when you have a moment or two to spare, attempt the contralateral version of standing still, which is to say, stand like our temple sculptures, or borrow from Indian classical dance.

Every classical dance form in our country is full of contralateral movements. In yoga, there are asanas such as the Nataraja-asana, which is a classic contralateral pose.

It does not need to be this pose. Any movement where you stretch the arm and leg in opposite direction is good enough. If everything else fails, swing your hands and legs and walk.

18

Drink Water like Indians Do

AN EARLY MEMORY OF my grandfather is of him holding a heavy lota (a small drinking vessel, with a lip) high above his head and pouring water into his mouth like a waterfall. He didn't lower his hand or close his mouth until the water finished. He had learnt—perhaps as a child—to drink water with his mouth open. This is something that every Indian either does or has observed. In traditional Indian households, people don't like to sip water straight from tumblers, lotas or glasses, as it is viewed as 'dirty', impure.

Today most of us have adopted Western ways and utensils. We sip from cups instead of pouring from on high, using tumblers. As for the lota, which was celebrated by Charles and Ray Eames as arguably the greatest, the most beautiful[1] designed object in India, has gone the way of antiques, and is being used as a decorative object rather than a utilitarian object. The Eames' report on India notes, 'Of all the objects we have seen and admired during our visit to India, the Lota, that simple vessel of everyday use, stands out as perhaps the greatest, the most beautiful.'

People showcase and display lotas in their living rooms or use them to grow plants. This is a pity.

Here is a thought: How about pulling out those heavy bronze or brass lotas that are lying in your grandmother's cupboard, and use them for what they were designed for: to store and drink water. The benefits are threefold.

1. You will flex your arm muscles when you lift these heavy objects.

2. You will have to pay attention when you pour the water down your throat like a waterfall and swallow, giving you a moment of mindfulness.
3. Most importantly, your head will fall back when you drink water, allowing it to hold a pose that is the opposite of the looking down we do through the day (when we text on smartphones), thus engaging different muscles.

19

Stand like an Eagle

THE FIRST THING THAT falters as you grow older is balance. Ironically, it is also the very thing you need to cultivate. Countless yoga poses involve standing on one leg, but why not do this while you are engaged in mundane activities such as brushing your teeth?

For the last year, I have stood in the Garudasana (eagle pose) while I brush my teeth. My legs are twisted together just like it happens in Garudasana, except I do a variant. I don't use my hands for the yoga pose. Instead, I use my left (non-dominant) hand to brush my teeth and lift the other arm up straight, looking somewhat like the Statue of Liberty crossed with a yoga pose that just so happens to be brushing her teeth.

Doing this offers many benefits. I have to balance on one leg. The twisting motion gives my legs a feeling of suppleness. An activity that is mundane and boring suddenly becomes a challenge as I have to concentrate on holding the balance.

You don't necessarily have to do this pose when you brush your teeth. You can balance on one leg using the Vrikshasana (tree pose); stretch one leg back and stand on the other, or squat and place one leg on the other. It is up to you. The goal is to stand on one leg for those few minutes.

There are three parts of the body that are used for balance: our eyes, our inner ears and our ankles. But now, we are such an eye-focused culture; we don't use the ears and the ankles. Simply closing your eyes and walking around once in a while helps. Somatic therapists say that being blindfolded for ten minutes activates long-dormant parts of the brain and changes how we react as we move through space.

20

Release Your Core Muscles

HOW DO YOU STAND? Do you lean forward or back? How do you walk? Do your feet lead? Do you use your core muscles (in the abdominal area) or the glutes (in the butt area)? Most important of all, do you use your psoas?

What is psoas, you may ask. It is a large muscle that connects the top part of your body to the bottom. It links the spine to the thighs. It helps you walk in the correct way, which is to walk in a fashion that creates a spinal twist; a gentle figure-eight movement of the hips that is created when you use your feet well.

As anyone who does yoga or is aware of their body knows, most of us lean slightly backwards while standing, causing our stomach area to jut out in front. When we walk, we do the same thing—we lean back a little, thus losing the most important part of the gait pattern, which is the spinal twist.

So, how can we correct this? There are many approaches. One is to watch how infants walk and try to mimic the way they hold themselves. I am a great fan of watching infants and toddlers to mimic their body movements for pretty much anything. The second approach is to be aware of our bodies, which is not possible in this age of looking at our smartphones while we move. So, ditch your phone while you walk. Pay attention to how you move. Figure out where the pain is in your body and then try to reduce it.

Part of what this book aims to do is to try to convince you that our bodies hold our emotions, and working with the body is one way of releasing these emotions. Toddlers do this naturally. They throw tantrums, roll on the ground and literally shake off their overwhelming emotions. A deer that has escaped a tiger's chase also shudders its way to normalcy. As adults, we feel our emotions in our body, especially in our gut and core. When we hear a bad news, experience grief and pain, or when we are afraid, our bodies reflect our feelings. Our breathing becomes shallow, and our core tightens. This chapter is about releasing these important core muscles in order to release stored emotions and pain. As an example, we look at the psoas.

Yoga teachers and pain professionals talk about releasing the psoas as a way of adjusting how you walk. Jonathan FitzGordon's *Psoas Release Party: Learn to Understand the Feeling and Healing of Your Pain!* talks about how to first figure out what and where your psoas is, and how to release it.

Most physiotherapists talk about the psoas in almost mystical terms because it is hard to reach or feel. It is buried deep within the body and, like all muscles, is also engaged in habitual (and sometimes wrong) patterns of posture depending on how you hold your body. Yes, the psoas stabilizes your stance, but more than that, it perceives danger and comfort. Like all deep tissues, it reflects and embodies our deep urges to survive and flourish. I have read a dozen articles that connect the psoas to yoga poses and emotion. Here is a compilation of what they say:

> Buried in the body, engaged in habitual patterns of holding (especially when you're sitting or standing), and deeply linked to your emotions, the psoas is best approached with quiet attention, patience, and perseverance. Awareness is the first key. Like a flashlight that illuminates the contents of a dark closet, you can use your attention to clarify and define each sensation in your core.[1]

Stretches to access the psoas involve all movements that make the front of our body arch backwards—like Kapotasana (pigeon pose), Ustrasana (camel pose), and Chakrasana (wheel pose). All of these will help you feel that muscle in your glute area.

Here is one simple way to release your psoas. Stand with one leg on a step and dangle the other leg. Just try it. The dangling leg pulls down on the psoas, thus releasing it and relaxing the hips. Do the same with the other leg.

You will be doing one of the biggest muscles in your body a big favour. There are other important core muscles as well; the idea here is to become aware of them.

21

Do One Thing to Help Your Diet

As a child, my parents used to call my throat a needle. '*Oosi thondai*,' they used to say disapprovingly, referring to the slowness with which I ate. I was painfully thin at that time and ate agonizingly slowly. Attending weddings was torturous for my family. Guests were served the wedding feast, seated group by group. When one group finished, the area was cleaned, new banana leaves, tumblers and katoris laid out; and the next group was invited to eat. I ate so slowly that I would eat across two 'pandhis' or groups. This continued all the way through adulthood.

When I joined college, I had to eat fast to ensure that all the good items on the college menu didn't run out. So nowadays, I have become a fast-eater and have the reverse problem: I have to force myself to eat slowly.

Studies link slow eating with satiety, the crucial feeling that tells us to stop eating. A 2015 Pubmed study called 'Effects of eating rate on satiety: A role for episodic memory?'[1] states that eating slowly caused participants to report greater fullness, not just at the end of the meal but also during intervals between meals. It typically takes us twenty minutes to experience satiety, which is another way of saying that it takes a while for your stomach to send 'full' signals to your brain to then command you to stop eating. I remind myself of this when I am ravenously hungry.

'*Hara hachi bun me*,' I tell myself. This is a Japanese phrase that tells us to eat until we are 80 per cent full. It became popular because of the

Okinawans of Japan, who have the highest percentage of centenarians: people over 100 years old. As described by numerous studies and books, including *The Okinawa Way: How the World's Longest-Lived People Achieve Everlasting Health and How You Can Too* by Bradley J. Willcox, Craig D. Willcox and Makoto Suzuki, a key aspect of longevity and health has to do with calorie-restriction. The Okinawans practise eating less using ageless proverbs such as, 'Eight parts of a full stomach sustain the man; the other two sustain the doctor,' to help them stop scarfing down their local favourites from Okinawa.

There are a few things you can tell yourself to reduce the speed with which you consume your food, particularly at home. The first thing to do is internalize the fact that the food is not going to disappear (like at your college hostel or mess). The second thing is to force yourself to pause. Make conversation, put your fork or spoon down, and look around the table. Remember how you used to eat as a baby. Watch babies if you don't remember. They take a bite, look around, play with the spoon, gurgle and generally drive the mother-in-a-hurry nuts to the point where the parent begins to force-feed the child, thus (you could say) setting it up for a lifetime of speed-eating.

A nice trick is to pace yourself with the slowest eater at the table. It could be a child; it could be that voluble guest at the other end of the table who talks more than he eats. No matter; remind yourself to take another spoonful only when the garrulous, slow-eating guest is taking one.

I find that another simple technique helps me slow down: breathing deeply. I find that if I stuff my mouth and breathe deeply at the same time, I have to pause to expel the breath before taking the next mouthful.

Eating slowly allows the stomach to catch up with the frequency at which you feed yourself each bite. When you are full, your stomach sends signals to your mouth to stop eating. The problem is that we eat so fast that we don't allow these signals to come through, until it is too late.

Take a breath. Count to five between every spoon. Keep a fund of jokes that you can entertain the table with. Whatever your way is, keep in mind that you must eat slowly. Now that I have sped up on the dining table, I pace myself with the slowest eater. That's the only way I can slow down.

Diets come and diets go. No matter which diet you follow—keto, paleo, vegan, or OMAD (one meal a day)—eating slowly enhances and catalyzes the effect.

22

Work on Your Vagus Nerve

IN 1994, AMERICAN PSYCHOLOGIST, Stephen Porges, introduced the poly-vagal theory which talked about how the vagus nerve helped with emotional regulation, social connection and the fear response. In simple terms, his theory was that improved vagal tone via learning to work with the vagus nerve helped us stay even-keel and deal with stress.

Over the years, this theory has been embraced by medical and mind-body practitioners who devised ways to regulate your nervous system. Cardiologist Dr Pradip Jamnadas, M.D., who founded and is medical director of Cardiovascular Interventions clinic in Florida is one of them. In his popular YouTube channel,[1] which goes by his name, Dr Jamnadas talks about how improved vagal tone, i.e., activating the vagus nerves, gives a whole host of benefits, including reducing inflammation, better gut health and reduced blood pressure. He also gives a list of hacks to help us get there, which drew me to his channel. But first, some facts.

The vagus nerve is the tenth cranial nerve originating in the brain stem (the medulla oblongata that we all mugged up about in high-school biology). It is the longest cranial nerve crucial for the parasympathetic nervous system. It causes the rest-and-digest mode of our bodies, as opposed to the sympathetic nervous system, which activates the fight-or-flight mode. As its name implies, the vagus nerve is a vagabond, affecting pretty much everything in our bodies, including digestion, heart rate and immune response. Having a good vagal tone means that our body knows how to relax, which is crucial for the repair work that needs to happen against stress. So, how do we improve vagal tone? Dr Jamnadas lists a whole range of options.

1. Humming relaxes you, which is why our Indian Bhramari breathing, when done before bed, will give you better sleep. Singing is great. Laughter yoga works.
2. Dunking your head into a bowl of ice and taking an ice bath is a method propagated by Wim Hof, the Dutchman who has created a Wim Hof[2] method of breathing with many adherents throughout the world, including me.
3. Valsalva, a manoeuvre that is practiced during scuba-diving helps.
4. Pretending that you are breathing into a balloon helps.
5. Massaging your neck and eyeballs softly

There are many more. Read the book, *Accessing the Healing Power of the Vagus Nerve* by osteopath Stanley Rosenberg (who, by the way, teaches osteopaths at the Sri Sri Ravishankar center for osteopathy), for simple exercises to improve vagal tone and thus, wellbeing.

How do you know if your vagal tone is better? You will experience sighing, swallowing or salivation, both of which are good. Check out a study, 'Vagal Afferent Activation Induces Salivation and Swallowing-Like Events in Anesthetized Rats', which states that 'Vagal afferent stimulation significantly increased salivation and swallowing-like events in a frequency-dependent manner.'

Here is another way to stimulate salivation, which is considered an indication of vagal tone. I found this through a 2020 study called 'Salivary Secretion and Salivary Stress Hormone Level Changes Induced by Tongue Rotation Exercise'.[3] The exercises described in the study are two: pretend to chew and rotate your tongue on the inside of your cheeks. Both make you salivate. Both help increase vagal tone. Naturally, I do this tongue rotation and hum at the same time, which is double the benefit, right?

Caveat: Some scientists don't agree with how Porges came up with his theory, even though they all agree that the vagus nerve is important.

23

Try Oil-Pulling

IT IS ALMOST NOON, but the corridors of Vasudeva Vilasam, an Ayurvedic hospital in Kerala, are blessedly dark and cool. I follow a nurse into various rooms where patients with asthma, arthritis and psoriasis are lounging in beds before or after their treatments. Many of them come here as a last resort, says the nurse, after they discover allopathy is unable to help them. The treatment rooms are quite large, with a massage table made of jackfruit in the centre. The air is redolent with neem, eucalyptus and camphor.

I spent summers in Kerala at my grandparents' ancestral home. My grandfather, a Western-trained doctor, prescribed pills to his patients but routinely got Ayurvedic massages himself. This layering of Western and Indigenous, the ancient and the modern, is nothing new or surprising in India, where sacred cows still stroll between glass-and-steel high-rises and several centuries coexist in cacophonous harmony.

Ayurveda originated in India over 5,000 years ago. It has a special resonance in Kerala, where it seems as woven into daily life as Kerala's potent toddy, curry leaves and fish-based cuisine.

Bordered by the Arabian Sea and blessed with a tropical climate, many of the herbs that Ayurveda prescribes grow easily in Kerala. Tulsi or holy basil, for instance, is revered in Ayurveda for its phlegm-reducing properties. Whenever I got a cold, my grandmother gave me honey tea with a Tulsi leaf floating on top.

The oil massages that Ayurveda recommends are part of daily life here. Women in Kerala massage coconut oil on their bodies and scalp before taking a bath. Even today, when the monsoon lashes the plentiful coconut trees, a part of the state pauses to undergo 'panchakarma' or rejuvenation therapies that include massages, herbal medicines and a special diet.

Ayurveda stresses prevention and has various simple and easy preventative techniques that people must do daily. Ayurveda calls these daily disciplines 'dinacharya'. 'Oil pulling' is one of them, along with candle gazing or 'trataka' and nasal rinse or 'neti'. I end up doing oil pulling, not daily but once a week or periodically. Oil pulling is a way to preserve dental hygiene. There are two methods called 'kavala' and 'gandusha'. They are broadly similar in how medicated oil is swirled within the mouth. In kavala, the oil is held in the mouth till the eyes tear and there is nasal discharge. In gandusha, the mouth is filled with three-fourths medicated oil, swirled and then spat out. Both methods follow the same protocol, and this is broadly what I have adopted.

I use sesame oil, which Ayurveda calls 'tila-thaila'. Sesame oil is prized in Ayurveda for being suited for various body types and temperaments.

Oil pulling sounds simple but is hard to do. The protocol is as follows:

- Do it before you brush your teeth.
- Do it first thing in the morning.
- Take a little sesame oil and pour it into your mouth. A tablespoon to start.
- Balloon out your cheek muscles and start swirling the oil within your mouth for five minutes.
- As you do this, you will find that your mouth secretes phlegm, thus watering down the oil.
- You may find that your eyes begin to water as well. There may be nasal discharge. All of this is good. It indicates that the oil is literally pulling out the toxins and impurities in your body.
- After five minutes, spit out the oil.
- Rinse your mouth with warm water with a pinch of salt.
- Brush your teeth.

- If you cannot do it for five minutes the first time, begin with one minute and gradually increase the time.

On the days that I do this, I find an unexpected side benefit: I sleep like a baby. Maybe it is because of the sinuses in my head getting a 'massage', or due to exercising the nerves in my mouth and face. Whatever the reason, oil pulling works for me.

24

Close Your Eyes When You Walk Inside

As I TYPE THIS, I am balanced on a giant ball the colour of a scalded tomato. It is called an exercise ball, but I use it as a chair in front of my computer console. The thing about this exercise ball chair is that I am permanently on the verge of falling off. It is constantly rolling, and consequently, my 'core' (as those exercise friends call it) is making adjustments. It is somewhat like a belly dancer in slow motion sitting on a chair on steroids.

I am moving and typing and moving and typing, which you might say explains the prose. After two weeks on this contraption, I can report a few things. One, getting up from a ball is different from getting out of a chair. With a chair, you push back and rise. Try that with a ball, and you will fall backwards on the floor. Your kids will pity you, and your dog will lick your nose.

The other thing that will happen is that you will experience instability and, therefore, fear. Fear is an emotion that we rarely experience these days, and I am not sure that is a good thing. Perhaps this is the reason why all of us experience diffused anxiety—because we don't have the adrenaline rush that comes with the life-or-death fear that early humans faced.

Our human ancestors faced dangerous beasts and life-threatening fear. The good news was that once they escaped, they didn't have the constant 'slow puncture' type anxiety that permeates our lives today. They quite literally shook off the fear, which is what animals and children do when they are overwhelmed with emotion. So, these days, I shake off difficult emotions, but that requires another post.

I decided to embrace fear after watching my parents. This is how I do it. Naturally, it is linked to fitness.

Do you consider yourself fit? Can you take the stairs two at a time?

Hell, yeah, you say.

Okay, try this. Close your eyes and take the stairs two at a time. Gets difficult, doesn't it?

Close your eyes and take the stairs one at a time.

Hold the bannister, close your eyes and walk down the stairs.

Walk around your home with your eyes closed.

As you get older, your eyesight and balance reduce. You also develop a fear of falling. One way to counter this is to get used to walking with closed eyes. This expands your 'proprioceptive capacity'. Proprioception is the awareness of your body in space. It is used to develop balance. When you walk with your eyes closed, you are forced to develop this proprioceptive capacity.

Embracing fear is uncomfortable. Walking around blind is both scary and uncomfortable. However, either may happen as you age. Those of us who cultivate skills to deal with this diminishing capacity that comes with ageing will be better prepared for that eventuality.

Closing your eyes for a few seconds a day is simply that practice. Consciously cultivating your proprioceptive ability is a happy by-product of closing your eyes.

Both of these will help you as you get older.

25

Seed Yourself with Fenugreek

THERE ARE TWO TYPES of people in the world: those that believe in alternative therapies and those that don't. In my family, I have both types. The scientific folks will not adopt anything that isn't proven with a double-blind study. In the second camp are those who hate taking allopathic drugs. In case you didn't realize it already, I am inclined towards the second camp. I view alternative therapies with an extremely open mind, although I do pop pain, fever and cold medicines when needed.

Now, what I am going to say in this chapter is an alternative therapy so, if you are suspicious of these, please skip ahead.

Think of the humble fenugreek or *methi* seed, famed in Ayurveda for improving lactation among new mothers and hair quality among women—and men. This is why your grandmother ground up fenugreek seeds and slathered it on your hair as a child: so that you could get lustrous locks. And this is why we soak fenugreek seeds in water overnight—if possible, in a copper pot—and drink it first thing in the morning. These days, I use fenugreek seeds, not on my hair but on my forehead.

At night, just before I go to bed, I sprinkle some fenugreek seeds in the space between my eyebrows and keep them in place using a Band-Aid. Since I sometimes wrap my oiled hair with a towel at night, the effect of the Band-Aid on my forehead underneath a white towel looks like a turban gone ghastly wrong. No matter. My goal is to press my third eye into submission, or rather flowering.

What prompted this exercise was a 2022 study called 'Efficacy of Su Jok Seed Therapy in Migraine: A Randomized Placebo-Controlled

Study'.[1] It concluded that the 'Su Jok seed therapy reduced the severity, duration and frequency of migraines, which in turn reduced the amount of painkillers consumed and the HIT-6 scores of patients with migraines'.

Before I come to what Su Jok is, let me explain why this study got me into seed therapy. Many days, I woke up with a heavy, groggy head. I attributed it to not sleeping well but wasn't sure how to fix it. So, I tried putting the fenugreek seeds (considered cooling) on my ajna chakra or the kundalini point between the eyebrows. After a few nights, I discovered happily that I woke up feeling lighter in the head. Maybe it was the power of suggestion, maybe it was the placebo effect, or maybe it was the seeds doing their work.

This 'third eye' point between the two eyebrows is powerful in most healing systems. It is supposed to stimulate the pituitary 'master' gland. The Chinese call this point 'yin-tang', and it has a powerful effect on sinus headaches and facial rejuvenation. Some acupuncture practitioners needle this point to reduce wrinkles. Hindu women wear their bindis over this point. Pressing seeds—mustard, fenugreek, peppercorns—over this point helps stimulate the master gland of our body, according to the ancients.

Seed therapy is based on two interesting concepts. One, it believes that the whole body can be condensed into the hands or feet. Specific locations in our hands and feet correspond to different organs. The thumb, for example, is considered to be the head. Placing two flax seeds or grains of rice just below the top of the thumb—where the eyes would be in the head—will help relax the eyes after a long day staring at the computer. You can keep them in place with a cello-tape or Band-Aid and sleep overnight with them.

So, where did seed therapy originate? This is hard to say, but it has flowered in Korea, where the late Professor Park Jae Woo, who passed away in 2010, created its tenets and concepts a few decades ago. Su Jok (the word means hands and feet) uses acupuncture, acupressure and seeds to create wellness. The International Sujok Association, with its own website 'sujok.com', is based in Nagpur, Maharashtra, so clearly

India has a lot of adherents to this method. The overarching theme is called 'zones of correspondences', by practitioners: larger body areas are linked to smaller ones. The hands, feet and ears are most potent, and the whole body can be plotted on them.

Second, seed therapy uses the notion of 'Like cures like', or 'Similia similibus curantur', as they say in Latin. Walnuts are good for the brain because they resemble the brain. Kidney beans, for example, are supposed to help the kidneys, so presumably, if you have a kidney stone, you could bandage a few kidney beans over the area in your feet or hands which relate to the kidneys. Some sleep overnight with these seeds strapped on, while others take them off after twenty minutes.

In terms of what seeds to use, it is up to you. Larger seeds can be used for larger organs (Sitaphal seeds for the stomach; plum seeds for the intestines) and smaller for the smaller organs. I've noticed that the seeds blacken and shrivel after use. Then again, I am a believer in these systems. Even if you are not, what do you have to lose?

At night, just before sleep, massage your ears with a bit of cream. It is deeply relaxing. Plus, the ears are one of the zones of correspondence in healing. Auriculotherapy (ear therapy) centres on finding points on the ear that correspond to the organs in the body. Massage your hands. If you find any tender point, that is where you put a small seed and make it stay in place using medical tape. Sleep well, and see if you feel better the next morning. Seeds, after all, are pure potential holders of the life force. They are the 'beeja' of life.

26

Lie on a Couch to Generate Ideas

THERE IS A REASON why psychologists like to put their subjects on the couch. When you are lying down and daydreaming, you reach into your psyche and touch aspects of your thoughts that are generally not on the surface. You connect to the parts of the brain that trigger creativity, insight and intuition. Most of us leave creativity and insight to chance, believing it will happen when we least expect it—such as in the shower. While that does happen, it can also be engineered.

Take the examples of Salvador Dalí and Thomas Edison. The former was the foremost surrealist artist who painted images of melting clocks. Edison popularized the use of electricity, including the light bulb. These were serious dudes, in other words, and were in the business of creating ideas. Did they leave idea generation to chance? Hardly.

Dalí had a way of napping that might seem odd to most of us. He would lie on his couch and let his mind wander. In his hands, he held a set of keys. Underneath the keys was a plate that was turned upside down. As his body relaxed, he would slowly fall asleep, right? Except he couldn't. Just as he nodded off, his hand would relax and the keys would clatter down on the plate and make a loud noise, thus waking him up. Most of us would be annoyed at the sound just as we were nodding off. Dalí engineered it.

He believed that this point between sleep and awakening was the fountainhead of new ideas, or in his case, images for paintings. When awakened by the clatter of keys, he would quickly record whatever images he had in his mind at the moment, then use them for his paintings. They sold for millions of dollars and helped popularize surrealism.[1]

A similar story applies to Edison, except legend has it that he held a set of metal ball bearings in his hand. When he dozed off, the ball bearings would clatter on an aluminium plate and wake him up. Like Dalí, Edison would record whatever insights he could recall from his unconscious brain and use them for his research.

There is a word for this stage when you are right at the point between being fully awake and being fully asleep. It is called hypnagogia. There is even a 1987 book on it, *Hypnagogia: The Unique State of Consciousness Between Wakefulness and Sleep* by Andreas Mavromatis.

In the book, the author makes the case that hypnagogia is the state where the brain's rational, logical and linguistic parts soften and relax. This is when the older, more ancient part of our brain—that thinks in myths, imagery and symbolism rather than in words and well-developed ideas—comes to play.

Usually, in our lives, the prefrontal cortex dominates our brain, giving us logic and rationality. All of this falls apart in the hypnagogic state. We are returned to a dream-like state that sets our minds loose. Hallucinogens also induce this effect, which is probably why many artists use them.

A 2022 article in *Harvard Medicine* titled 'Behind the Veil of Hypnagogic Sleep'[2] states that in the hypnagogic state, the mind makes associations between what we would consider random ideas: essential for writing poetry, creating art and composing music. Freed from logic, the mind uses imagination to come up with new solutions. The good news is that this hypnagogic state is accessible to all of us without the use of hallucinogens. All we need to do is train ourselves to wake up pretty much as we fall asleep, using keys, metal balls, bells, or whatever it is that will clatter and make a sound.

I use my silver anklets. They are light and easy to hold as I nod off on the couch. When my hands relax, they loosen and fall on the ground, making a musical jingling sound. Not that I have any genius-like flashes of insight, but sometimes, a knotty problem that I have been wrestling with solves itself.

The title character of the American television series *The Mentalist* is a super-smart psychic named Patrick Jane, who solves crimes using a combination of observation, memory and intuition. He insists that a couch be laid out in his office at the FBI because lying on the couch gives him clues and insights that don't normally occur to other detectives.

While your boss might not agree to have a couch in your office, you can lie on one at home when you are working on a serious problem. Who knows your reinvigorated mind will turn into an idea-generation machine? After all, it may persuade your boss to put a couch in the common area of your office.

Naps are in. Top executives are raving about how a twenty-minute nap makes them stay productive longer. Most animals nap and wake up throughout the twenty-four-hour cycle. This is called polyphasic sleep (many phases of sleep and awakening). Humans used to do this, too, but now we are biphasic sleepers. We sleep during the night and (try to) stay awake during the day. Mid-afternoon, when our energy dips, some of us take a siesta.

Spanish cultures still do this and return to work, revived. Politicians are great power nappers. Just look at TV coverage of the Parliament to see how many of them nod off during the proceedings.

Winston Churchill, Ronald Reagan and Bill Clinton, among others, used to take a power nap in the middle of the day. Most of us nap only when we are exhausted or sleep-deprived. The trick is to teach yourself to nap at will, typically in the middle of the day when your mind and body are drained.

There are many views about how long to nap. What is the optimal time for a power nap? Can you believe that people actually debate these things? The consensus, however, is about twenty minutes. Half an hour is too long, and ten minutes will not.

Throughout the centuries, inventors and artists have plotted how to get their creative muse to stay on. Or at least appear consistently. So, go ahead. Lean back and go horizontal. Hold a keychain in your hand and dream—and see where it leads you.

27

Stare at the Horizon When You Walk

WHERE DO YOU LOOK when you walk? Okay, don't tell me. I do it too. I check messages on the phone when I walk.

Here is a suggestion. Don't just look up when you walk. Look at the horizon. It is how early *Homo sapiens* walked. Thcy scanned the horizon, searching hither and thither for animals or other danger. Staring at one spot is a new accomplishment in human evolution. Staring at a small screen is just a generation old. Our eyes are adapting rapidly to this evolutionary unnatural habit. If you want to relax your eyes, revert to those ways of seeing that our eyes are used to, i.e., looking at the horizon.

These days, when I walk in the city, and remember doing this, I look at the farthest point I can see. I scan the horizon, moving my gaze from left to right. I look at clouds and try to keep my eyes as soft as them.

We don't realize how much tension we store in our eyes, face and jaw. Soften and loosen is a good mantra as you walk and stare at the horizon.

28

Bless the Giver

IT IS THE WEIRDEST piece of advice that I have been given, but it worked. When my daughter was four, she used to throw terrible tantrums, usually at twilight after a long day—for both of us.

It would begin with me trying to feed her and her refusing to eat. Quickly it would degenerate to tears, cries of 'No, no', followed by loud wails and rolling on the floor. I would lock myself in the bathroom, just so I would not slap my child.

One evening, at my wit's end, I called my mother. I told her that I didn't know what to do to calm my child down. 'Bless her,' said my mother. 'Just think to yourself, "Bless you", when she goes into tantrum mode.'

Like that is going to work, I thought skeptically. But I didn't have any options so I began repeating this quietly when my daughter had a meltdown.

'Bless you! Bless you!'

It didn't seem to calm her down, but it calmed me instead, which was perhaps the point.

Shanti is a Sanskrit term which means peace. 'Om Shanti, Shanti, Shanti,' ends a popular verse co-opted by yoga studios globally. In Hinduism, offering peace even to your enemies is a way to calm things down. When animals were sacrificed in the Vedic age, the person slaughtering the animal whispered words of peace and love to it before the act. The slaughterers were called 'samitrs'. The word 'samitr' has multiple meanings, one of which is '[he] who keeps his mind calm'.[1] Such a person is in a position to say words of peace and love, when chaos reigns.

In my own home, I began whispering 'bless you' when I felt like slapping my kids. On good days, when I remember to, I take this to the next level. I bless (which is another way of thanking) anyone from whom I receive an offering, be it a samosa or a glass of wine. I look at the bartender and silently bless him for giving me sustenance—which is what a cocktail is at the end of a long day. I'm not sure if this has any tangible effect, but it certainly makes me feel connected to the person giving me nourishment. More than that, it converts—at least in my head—food into a sacred substance. And it makes me feel good in the bargain.

29

Wear Banana Shoes

THESE DAYS, I PAD around the house wearing rocker bottom shoes. No kidding. Google this phrase and check if you like. They stand about twice as high as normal sneakers and have an underside shaped like a curved banana. When I first put them on, my husband asked if I was wearing prosthetics. In other words, these rocker bottom shoes aren't your average stiletto. Walking on them, though, is a breeze.

There are many brands that sell rocker bottom shoes these days. An early brand was MBT Shoes or Masai Barefoot Technology Shoes. The Swiss founder of MBT wanted to imitate the walk of the Masai tribesmen who walked barefoot across the soft, uneven earth of the Masai Mara.

It was a seductive idea because the Masai are one of the most graceful people on earth. That is ultimately what sold me on these shoes.[1] Have you ever seen a less-than-graceful Masai? I haven't. I haven't seen a Masai at close quarters at all, but even on TV or YouTube, all you see is elegance in the way they move.

The logic is that when we wear shoes, we walk in a way that doesn't allow us to use joints in our toes. Some walking experts call shoes 'bandage' for the feet. The idea is to use all thirty-three joints in the feet.

Our ancestors walked barefoot on uneven ground. Now we bandage our feet in shoes and walk on flat ground. This doesn't allow for joint movement in the toes. If you walk barefoot on uneven but soft ground, your body will constantly adjust to this natural instability and use more muscles in the process. In urban areas, however, we wear flat shoes on flat concrete ground, negating our body's ability to contract all those small, supportive muscles in response to natural instability. At least, that's the argument anyway.

Does it work? I think so. As it is, sitting on the ball-chair, I am feeling balanced. The added benefit is that both the ball and the shoe are the tipping point to exercise, which, is really my secret weapon. Picture this scenario: you are standing, waiting for the elevator, and your unstable shoe is making you sway from side to side. How hard can it be to increase that sway to a side stretch? That's what happens, both while sitting on the ball and walking around in my rocker shoes. I stretch during the day, pretty much unconsciously and without much production. It is, in a way, exercise nirvana. Or lack thereof. Okay, so what do you do if you don't have these shoes and don't want to buy them? You adapt their principles. You try walking on grass and sand barefoot. When inside your home, you try to use the joints of your feet by standing on your toes. You sway and stretch when possible, imagining yourself to be a Masai warrior crossing the African Savannah.

30

Touch the Earth

WHEN CAROLYN DAVIDSON DESIGNED the Nike swoosh logo for her accounting professor, Phil Knight, who had just founded a shoe company, she billed him $35 for her services. Knight said that he didn't love the logo but believed it would grow on him.[1] His comment reflects an essential paradox about the creative process: what someone deems as mediocre may become iconic. Conversely, someone who thinks it is good maybe poorly received.

I thought of this and other creative paradoxes as I tried to run barefoot through the grass. I am not a habitual runner. I own Nike running shoes with their swoosh, but I use them to hike, not to run. I may not run, but at least I have the right gear, I remind myself, just in case I am caught in the Sahara Desert and decide to go for a morning jog.

Running across the Sahara offers a chance to try the latest trend in fitness: barefoot running. My latest possession is a pair of five-fingers Vibram shoes, marketed as close-to-barefoot footwear. They fit like a second skin, but you cannot mistake them for skin—they're orange!

According to the research done by Harvard Professor Daniel Lieberman and his colleagues, human beings evolved to be long-distance runners, not sprinters. We are not good at sprinting. A domestic cat can outrun Usain Bolt. But we can run marathons and ultra-marathons, and many hardy souls do.

The question that has been tormenting runners, researchers and shoe manufacturers for the last few years is this: what are the right shoes for endurance running? Some say cushioned shoes and the other barefoot.

Barefoot runners eschew shoes. When you run in shoes, they say, the heel strikes first, with great force. Consider how often your heel strikes the ground when you run and you begin to comprehend the wear and tear. But when you run barefoot, the front of your foot, along with the lateral part, lands first. Your body adjusts so that the impact is less than when you wear shoes. You develop callouses, but injuries are pretty rare.

Now, if only these geniuses can invent a running shoe that simulates running without the actual act. That would make me leap, run and whoop in the air—all barefoot.

Today, most Indians are switching to footwear and resisting the natural feel of earth on feet. On his visit to India in 1938, late great Swiss psychologist Carl Jung was profoundly affected. He said,

> It is quite possible that India is the real world and that the white man lives in a madhouse of abstractions. Life in India has not yet withdrawn into the capsule of the head. It is still the whole body that lives. No wonder the European feels dreamlike; the complete life of India is something he merely dreams of. When you walk with naked feet, how can you ever forget the earth?[2]

This is a profound quote because it symbolizes the holistic attitude intrinsic to living in India. We don't differentiate between inside and outside, mind and body. We still continue to walk barefoot, which is good for the body and mind. Why not stick to it, I say. If you have a yard where you can walk barefoot, do it. Go ahead, touch the earth with your feet. You can always come back home and wash them.

31

Wobble While You Work

IN THE US, STANDING and walking desks are well-known and used by the rich and famous. The idea is to fit your laptop on a treadmill so you are continuously walking as you type. What can you do if you don't have the space or the inclination to buy these walking desks? Some options are a wobble board and a height-adjustable desk. But since I am all about moving, let me go with the wobble board.

A wobble board is a circular or rectangular platform with a ball underneath. You stand on it and, well, wobble till you don't because you have attained a Zen state of calmness where you are so centred and still that you can even walk on water or stand still on a board that wobbles. Physical therapists use this board to improve balance, core strength, stability and proprioception (a Latin word implying the connections between various body parts). When standing on the wobble board, the thinking is replaced with a focus on the mind.

Although that theory sounds, well, wobbly, it has precedent. Lots of geniuses have relied on movement for inspiration and focus. Apple's former CEO, Steve Jobs, famously took a walk to discuss ideas. Mark Twain paced while dictating his stories. Beethoven walked along the Danube River and through the woods for inspiration. Taming the body's nervous energy can seemingly help focus the mind. Perhaps there is a psychobiological element to creativity, and since mine can use all the help it can get, I decided to try this technique.

I ordered a wobble board (and you can get these for as low as Rs. 500 online). Mine is sleek and black, has a tactile roughness on top and wobbles satisfactorily. It took me twenty minutes to get used to the unsteadiness. After that, it was like standing on a swing, albeit a gently rocking one.

I am standing atop it as I type these words. After two hours, I feel the muscles in my ankles, calves and abdomen. After a day, I develop that achy feeling that comes after a workout, only—to my delight—without moving my feet.

Traditional wisdom suggests that using mind improves the body. For example, discipline and perseverance are key to getting fit; you stop yourself from gorging on calorific foods through mental discipline and force yourself to exercise everyday through sheer perseverance. Wobble boards work the same way.

In a lyrical article titled, 'Not Only Canaries Need Sing',[1] UK-based voice coach, Angela Caine talks about using a wobble board to help singers. The goal, she says, is to be able to stand still on it. This means that the body weight is balanced evenly between both legs, improving the voice. My physical therapist told me that my end goal was to stand on one leg on my Thera-Band, imitating the 'tree pose' in yoga.

So far, I haven't come close. I do my version of the tree pose by swaying from side to side, wobbling like an egg yolk. But, in the process, I have discovered muscles where I didn't think they existed. I don't know for sure if wobbling has improved my neural networks. My kids still think I am weird. But weird is good. Weird is one step away from creative.

Wobble boards are available everywhere. I got mine in India. I stand barefoot on it, get an acupressure-type massage, wobble a bit and type away. If the point is to force yourself to move, there is nothing like the danger of toppling over to prompt it.

32

Dictate into Your Phone

DO YOU DICTATE OR type your messages? What about emails? Today, every computer comes loaded with tools to transcribe speech to text. Every phone can listen to your voice and convert it to text. The question is: do you use it? If not, you should.

I began to try dictation mostly because my arms hurt when I typed. I was nervous about getting carpal tunnel syndrome, and the only options were either to hire a secretary, which I couldn't afford or to start talking to my computer. These days, the voice recognition software on most computers and the attached programmes are so good that you can dictate to your phone or computer.

I don't know if you are one of those people who can think in whole paragraphs. I am not. I stutter and stammer. My speech is liberally peppered with 'uhhh' and 'ummm' and other incomprehensible phrases. To dictate into a device, I have to gather my thoughts, slow them down, and streamline them into whole sentences. In fact, I am doing that now as I dictate this essay. It is a mobile app version of breathing in and out.

One breath, one thought, one sentence. Isn't that like meditation?

Thinking in sentences involves pausing and rehearsing the actual words that you want to say in your mind. To continue in this manner requires concentration in the face of a blinking device with the prompt 'record'.

Do this often enough, and you don't even have to sit in the lotus position and take calming breaths—because, you see, there is no point yelling at your dictation software for typing 'phrases' as 'freezes'. You have to take a deep breath and get the words out again. The calmer you are, the better it types.

33

Walk like a Tribal

WOULD YOU CARRY YOUR backpack on your head? It would help not just your aching back but also your posture.

Some years ago, *The New York Times* published an article titled, 'The Posture Guru of Silicon Valley.'[1] It featured a holistic health practitioner called Esther Gokhale. Trained in Harvard and Princeton, Gokhale is an acupuncturist and holistic health practitioner based in California. She studies ancient tribal societies and how they carry themselves. As her name suggests, she is half-Indian.

Gokhale links posture to health. She suggests that how we hold our spines and backs is key to determining whether we get backache. After observing how women in Indian villages walk, she recommends 'glide walking'.

In the jargon of somatic health specialists, this type of walk is broken down into the placement of the heel and leg. My two takeaways after watching her videos and reading her books are fairly simple:

a. Don't feel afraid to jut out your butt when you walk;
b. Pretend that you are holding a basket on your head when you walk.

If possible, *do* place whatever you are carrying on your head. It will force you to lift your head, hold your core, keep your back straight and walk from the hip, thus cultivating a beautiful figure eight, which walking specialists call the 'spinal twist'.

We can discount the jargon, but we can own the form. After all, it is common in India to carry weight on your head. Models do this by artificially placing books on their heads to cultivate a mincing walk. Mere mortals like us can imitate this in life.

If you are carrying a bag or backpack, place it on your head whenever possible. I do this when I am on an empty stretch of road or climbing up the stairs in my building. Once you get the hang of it, you will become emboldened to carry your backpack on your head. With this not only will your gait become more graceful, but your back will also thank you.

34

Gain Willpower without Moving an Inch

IN AN IDEAL WORLD, stilettos would have massager inserts in them. French fries would remove toxins from your body and shrink your waistline, and everyone would have the willpower to do whatever they wanted to accomplish. But reality, sadly, is a little different.

Social psychology points to four characteristics that lead to success: resilience, willpower, focus and imagination. In an outlandish and somewhat brilliant twist, all four of these characteristics can be cultivated by a practice that is at least as ancient as Indian corruption. I speak, of course, of the global juggernaut we call yoga.

As someone who learnt yoga as a child, I am a little unnerved by the sight of blonde women with long Scandinavian bodies chanting Sanskrit mantras and doing the downward dog with far more flexibility than I ever could. I should feel proud rather than resentful. After all, it takes a special kind of inventiveness to look at how scorpions, dogs, crows and locusts move and come up with asanas that manage to enlighten or humiliate, depending on what level you're at.

Like many Indian children, I was sent to the local playground to learn yoga from a man who looked like a military commander. My teacher made us contort our bodies into bends, stretches and lunges. No theory was given. Raps on the knuckles were a favoured mode of punishment, along with 'Stand up on the bench', except that there was no bench on the field, so it was modified to 'Hang by the branch', which was equally humiliating because we stood there swaying on a guava branch that was perpetually at risk of breaking (which if you read my previous chapter on wobble boards was how we all need to be standing anyway).

I have remained interested in yoga. I do the asanas or poses every now and then, sometimes consistently and sometimes sporadically, as is my nature, or shall we say, prakruti. Looking back, I turned to yoga at transition points in my life. As a newlywed, my husband would walk into the house and find me engaged in a headstand—an unnerving experience for him, particularly after a flaming row.

When things got rough in graduate school, I would wake up in the morning and do the trikonasana, or the triangle pose, bending down as if I was surrendering to a higher power—or, in my case, my thesis adviser. After the birth of my children, my gynaecologist recommended stretches. Although I couldn't see how stretching could remove stretch marks, I resumed yoga.

There are many schools of yoga now, and those of us who have learnt yoga since childhood have a view on them. For example, I don't subscribe to Bikram Yoga, in which practitioners do the asanas in a room heated to 40 degrees Celsius, with high humidity to boot. It's like a combination of sauna and steam shower, except that people are not naked and are doing poses.

Power yoga was invented in the US as a way of combining fitness with yoga. As someone who is reflexively against fusion—be it in food or anything else—I have trouble with this too. I find the Bihar School of Yoga (BSY) to be authentic; as are the Ashtanga, Sivananda and Iyengar schools.

My current teacher follows these four schools and we often have discussions. He recently taught me a Sanskrit quote, '*Sthiram sukham asanam*'. It comes from Patanjali's *Yoga Sutras*. The literal meaning being stable, still (sthiram), comfortable, relaxed (sukham), pose, posture (asana). If you find a pose in which you are able to stay still for a long time, it is like doing an asana. Hindu mythology supports this. In every mythical story, it seems, there is a sage (rishi) who sits in Padmasana (the lotus pose) for centuries in order to obtain immortality, the company of beautiful women, or eternal youth.

Why obtain immortality if you are going to use it to sit still for centuries is beyond me, but that was what the stories said.

My goals are more modest. I would like to have more willpower so that I can resist any number of things: stop eating bhujia sev and potato chips late at night; stop throwing things at the television when a particular news anchor comes on; and stop hankering for increased willpower to engage in all these goals.

Roy F. Baumeister, a psychologist and author of *Willpower: Rediscovering The Greatest Human Strength*, has a few pithy points. He says that willpower is a muscle. It can be developed, but it gets tired with overuse. So, if you want to stop eating chocolates at the end of the day, reduce the number of decisions you make in the beginning. A simple way to do this is to wear the same suit to work every day. Schools, airlines, hospitals, and the armed forces call it a uniform.

The logic is simple. Choices involve decisions which reduce willpower. One of the activities that Baumeister suggests is to sit still in one position. He says that postural discipline leads to mental discipline. In other words, use an asana (pose) to develop focus and willpower.

This, then, is the way to merge yoga with modern social psychology. Try sitting in one position without moving. It could be in front of the computer or while conversing with somebody. The whole point is to find a position where you can stay still and do just that.

According to Baumeister, this stillness increases willpower over time. '*Sthiram sukham asanam.*'

35

Use the Dual-n-Back App

A FRIEND OF MY children was visiting, and I told him, 'Thanks to your mother, I am drinking hot water these days. Like her, I too believe that the hot water will melt the fat globules in my body, and I will become slim, indeed svelte.'

I was chuffed with pride, having added one more trick to my arsenal of shortcuts. 'Ma,' she said, 'you've said the same thing four times in the last twenty-four hours. Don't you remember? I am getting worried about you.'

She didn't exactly call me senile, but the sympathetic looks on the faces of the five children sitting around the dining table implied it.

The kids were wrong, not about my memory, which is fallible, but about the reason for the repetition. I repeat myself endlessly, not because I am senile but because I haven't been heard.

On an average day, I give about a hundred instructions to my kids. Not a lot, I know, but I try to keep things simple in my household. I believe in giving my family freedom of choice so that they don't become completely dependent on me for everything. That said, I remain mildly shocked when I return from a trip and find that the house hasn't collapsed.

Every morning, I wake up and spell out instructions about bathing, dressing and homework. In response, I get an eyeroll. How do schoolteachers do it? How do they make sure that an entire classroom of kids has heard what they said?

There is, however, an essential, if disheartening, truth in what my daughter said. My memory is failing. I don't think it is age-related. My friend, Ayesha, is younger than me, and claims she can't remember anything. I think it has to do with neuroplasticity, but I didn't write this sentence just so that I could use that word.

And while on this topic, I have a piece of advice for all you smug, satisfied spouses who have never misplaced a thing: when your husband or wife comes to you with the question, 'Do you know where I left the car keys?', control the temptation to say, 'Think back to the time when you saw them last.'

This is what my husband tells me when I ask such a question. In a cosmic act of retribution, most forgetful folks are usually married to folks with excellent memories, who then proceed to 'help' them remember. But back to the question and answer, you may think you are being helpful, but you're not. If I could think back to when I last saw my library cards or car keys, I'd find them. I wouldn't be asking you.

Forgetfulness has something to do with age, but not entirely. I blame my forgetfulness on the genes I inherited from my absent-minded father. Modern research might be about to corroborate that.

A 2010 study in the *Journal of Politics* talked about a gene that predisposes people who seek out new experiences to be more liberal in their views. Naturally, the dreaded 'liberal gene' was immediately featured on Fox News with the sensational headline, 'Researchers Find the "Liberal Gene".'[1]

Meanwhile, a 2010 study by German researchers at the University of Bonn has identified a gene associated with altruism in people who give twice as much money to charitable causes as those without it.[2]

And if geneticists can isolate the gene that made me an impulsive eater and an empathetic socialist, why can't they discover the forgetfulness gene and, if possible, fix it?

There are many ways to improve memory, all of which I am trying. *The Mentalist*, a television show I used to be addicted to, talked about cultivating a 'memory palace', something that the 2011 book *Moonwalking with Einstein* explains.[3] Paying attention to your surroundings is important. The ancient yogic practice of trataka, or candle gazing, improves concentration.

Mindfulness practices and meditation centre the mind and improve memory. However, I needed something more doable than 'sit still and empty your mind of all thoughts'. An empty mind is a normal state of being for me. As for sitting still, if I could do that, I would have—paradoxically—conquered the world. I needed to feel like I was 'doing something' to improve my memory, not just sitting around doing nothing. I looked for help on the internet.

I found an app that claims to improve working memory. It is called Dual-n-Back, and it is a game that you have to play twenty times a day. There are many apps both on Android and iPhones that cater to Dual-n-Back. The one I like is called IQ Boost, and it is a game of squares that progressively becomes more difficult.

In a 2017 study, 'N-back Versus Complex Span Working Memory Training'[4], researchers found that playing Dual-n-Back for thirty minutes a day, five days a week, showed a 30 per cent improvement in their working memory. This was nearly double the gains made by the group working with the other common task, known as 'complex span'. The group playing Dual-n-Back also showed significant changes in brain activity in the prefrontal cortex, the critical region responsible for higher learning.

I have played this game for a week and can confidently say it has improved my working memory.

Now, where did I leave my spectacles?

36

Know Thyself

EVERY ANCIENT FAITH HAS a version of the above Greek quote. Since I am Hindu and a student of Sanskrit, I tried finding a Sanskrit word for self-reflection. One word that kept coming up was Vimarsha. It means self-reflection, and its most beautiful reflection comes from the Natya Shastra, a treatise on dramatics. Chapter 21[1] talks about the five junctures or sandhis of a dramatic play. One of the junctures is called Vimarsha-sandhi, which alludes to pausing to deliberate. And what does the actor deliberate on? They deliberate over the bija or seed that has sprouted in the garbha or womb due to some emotion such as anger, envy, distress or temptation.

This pretty much covers the trajectory of emotions and what to do with them. This helps me a lot when I get anxious. I am what psychologists call a maximizer and a catastrophizer. This means that no matter what the situation, I can do more. No matter what the situation, I think of the worst-case scenario. I spiral out of control, in other words.

How does this play out? I tend to assume the worst when I don't hear back from someone, whether it is a friend, colleague or interviewer. Not only do I think that they have rejected me, I also assume that they hate me and that they are whispering words of mockery to all my friends and converting them from being my friend into my enemy.

When my child is late, I think that someone has kidnapped her.

When a boss asks to see me, I think I am going to be fired.

You see how this is.

Age helps in this regard. As I get older, I feel that my anxiety has reduced. My imagination, too, has reined in. But the problem with age is that you must wait until you achieve it.

Vimarsha, or the pause, is a more active approach. Deliberating on the seed of the emotion along with slow breathing helps. Through this process, I have found much fear in my prakruti or constitution, which is why I imagine the worst. Fear is the seed of my emotions, and merely acknowledging it has helped calm them down.

A quote that is attributed to Swiss psychologist Carl Jung also helps. 'What you resist persists,' he is supposed to have said. On the flip side, what you accept dissolves.

Vimarsha is a method to process the seed and seat of emotions and to witness how they play out across the sandhis or junctures of the situation. It is a way to a better emotional outcome.

37

Learn to Juggle

RECENTLY, A FRIEND ASKED me an interesting question, 'Which would be the hardest addiction for humankind to shrug off? Sugar, Sitting or Smartphones?'

Giving up all three would make you productive and healthy—a kind of saint and Steve Jobs rolled into one. It is also a pipe dream.

Shaking off one of the scourges of modern life might be what myths call the 'hero's quest', i.e. the most arduous voyage. I know folks who have given up sugar for a year and survived. I know folks who have walking desks so that they don't sit. But I don't know anyone who has given up their devices for any significant amount of time, even though we all talk about going on a digital detox.

Figuring out your relationship with your phone is a challenging endeavour. But I would like to convince you that it is also necessary. Particularly in this age of AI and ChatGPT, which does everything for your brain, trying to think on your own is not just healthy; it may also be essential for your survival as a personal and professional, and I am only slightly exaggerating.

How do I do this? This is an intensely personal question because it involves figuring out your triggers. What makes you reach for the phone as a reflexive default? How can you stop yourself from reaching for the phone so that it doesn't become a punishment and require enormous willpower? My method has been to keep objects around that are pleasurable and also replace the phone. So, keep a notebook nearby and make lists on it instead of your phone. Learn to juggle. Not only will it improve your dexterity, but it will also calm you down.

Doodle. Do complex sequential movements that involve memory, which is another way of saying, learn to dance. Track how many times you reflexively pick up the phone every day and then try to cut it down. Silence notifications. Remove social media apps from your mobile device. Try to write out the outline of your speech on a piece of paper before reaching straight for the device to type it in.

It doesn't matter what you do or how you do it. It only matters *that* you do it.

38

Become Friends with Local Herbs

HOW MANY DAYS CAN you go before you crave the foods of your childhood? I can last two weeks, tops, and only if I am stuck in the middle of the Australian outback without access to turmeric or some decent curry powder. When it comes down to it, most of us are pretty narrow in terms of our food preferences. We may have cultivated a taste for sushi and noodles but scratch the surface, and we each have our own versions of shepherd's pie, cheeseburger and fries or, in my case, rasam and dosa.

Food is intimately tied to identity, home, memory and well-being. We may each have acquired global preferences in other parts of our lives, but take food away, and you will have the skeletal remains of the global sophisticates that we've all become. All this is a preamble to describe the deepest, most primal taste of all, one that infants instinctively gravitate towards. I speak, of course, of the sweet taste of sugar.

In a cruel cosmic paradox, we are now learning that the sweetness we all love is bad for us. There are herbs called 'madhunashini' that can numb our tongues so we don't taste sweets. Diabetic supplements abound in the Indian market.

A 2014 American documentary, *Fed Up*,[1] calls sugar a 'weapon of mass destruction'. It takes a hard-hitting look at how sugar and processed foods have permeated diets globally. It is a vicious cycle. As countries get richer, sugar intake doubles. People eat more processed food, and the odds of getting type 2 diabetes increases. According to the documentary, exercising is not enough to stave this off.

What really should happen is a return to the way of eating practised by our parents and grandparents. To paraphrase author Michael Pollan's[2] famous quote, 'Eat food, not too much, mostly plants', we should eat whole foods, mostly vegetables, in small quantities.

Eating local herbs such as amritavalli, madhunashini, neem and moringa leaves is a good way to stave off sugar cravings. A single amritavalli leaf or a handful of tender moringa leaves is enough. Amritavalli means 'creeper with amrita' (or nectar of immortality); its benefits are well-documented in Ayurveda. Look up Tinospora cordifolia, also known as Guduchi or Giloy. Similarly, eating tulsi with ghee and rice is something our grandparents did. Moringa is now a global sensation, but in south India, murungai keerai adai (a thick dosa) is a delicacy. So walk around your garden, or visit the sabzi mandi, make friends with herbs.

39

Use Self Control—the App, That Is

An earlier chapter was about getting away from your smart device. This is a subset of that goal dealing with that time-sink we call 'social media'.

Social psychologist Jonathan Haidt's 2024 book, *The Anxious Generation*[1] links anxiety and mental illness amongst teens to a 'phone-based childhood' versus a 'play-based childhood'. Controlling how much time we spend on the phone is key to good physical and mental health. This we know. I have tackled this in two ways. One, by linking the reward of scrolling through Instagram on my phone to an action that is good for me: an exercise. The other is what I talk about here.

How much time do you spend on Instagram, Facebook or X? No, seriously: is it an hour a day or minutes spread over the day?

And why do you go there? Is it to bond with friends, check on how and what they are doing, or to surf and stalk people for vicarious pleasure? Or is it all of the above, like it is for me? Psychologists have three pieces of advice for folks like us: Get a life. Break it off. Stop right now.

The side effects of increased social media usage have become the topic of several academic papers. For instance, German researchers have found that envy is the predominant emotion aroused via Facebook. Their 2013 study points to an 'envy spiral' that happens to all of us after we get on social media.[2] Seeing our friends' awards, travel plans, photographs, fabulous daily routines and children can make us jealous. This makes sense: the things that most people post on their Insta story are the highlights of their lives, and not what broadcast journalists call the 'B-roll'.

People don't post the mundane minutiae of daily life, not the ups and downs, and not the large chunks of boredom that constitute life, even a life well-lived. My question is a little different: are we so interested in sharing our lives online that we forget to enjoy them? Are we so busy trying to document our lives that we fail to live them?

I am as guilty of this as anybody else. I see something beautiful, and I immediately want to photograph it and post it on Instagram. I read a well-researched article and immediately want to share it with my friends on LinkedIn to humble-brag about my taste in reading. I watch a funny movie and immediately want to tell my followers on X to do the same.

The act of sharing is not bad; it improves human enjoyment. But in the past, sharing had its time and place. You attended a party; people would be talking about the movies; you would tell them about the latest thriller that you enjoyed. But all this happened after the fact, after you watched the movie, not during it. Does all our instant, live and constant sharing have consequences? I believe so.

Viewing the world through the prism of social media causes you to pay selective attention. Instead of experiencing a performance, you photograph it and post it on Instagram. Instead of reading about neuroscience in a blog, you read the first few paragraphs, deem it share-worthy and send it along to your followers on X. You see a design blog that you like, and before you even make sure that the content is at all suitable, you share it on Facebook. The act of sharing makes you appear erudite and engaged, but over time, it can diminish your enjoyment.

So, what to do? Find ways to help yourself. Hide your phone for a while. Switch it off. Take a walk without it. Go to a party promising yourself that you won't check your phone. Or find an app to help you. Yes, I see the irony of using an app on your phone to help you detach from it.

There are apps that help keep track of and control the amount of time we spend on social media. They keep a tab on how we use our time on the computer. But only we can judge if time off our devices is a goal worth having.

40

Quantify Yourself

WARNING: THE LINES BELOW were spoken by a real person:

> I got up this morning at 6:10 a.m. after going to sleep at 12:45 a.m. I was awakened once during the night. My heart rate was 61 beats per minute—my blood pressure, 127 over 74. I had zero minutes of exercise yesterday, so my maximum heart rate during exercise wasn't calculated. I had about 600 milligrams of caffeine, zero of alcohol. And my score on the Narcissism Personality Index, or the NPI-16, is a reassuring 0.31.[1]

No, this isn't a robot; giving you a detailed account of its activities and body specifications. It was part of a speech given by Gary Wolf at a 2010 TED Talks conference. Wolf and his partner, Kevin Kelly, were editors at *Wired* magazine. They coined the term 'quantified self', which means a 'collaboration of users and tool makers who share an interest in self-knowledge through self-tracking'.

In plain English, this means figuring out if what you are telling yourself is true. If you actually exercised for forty-five minutes or just thought you did, if you ate two dosas or just assumed that you did in the heat of the discussion you were having with your colleagues. It is using apps and devices to be your bullshit detector.

Today, the quantified self has become a movement with forums and conferences where thousands of giddy quantifiers gather to share data about their body weight and bowel movements.

The quantified movement makes sense. Just the act of observing what you eat will make you eat less. Just keeping track of how many scoops of ice cream you are downing will make you take one spoon less. Keeping track of how much you weigh will help you monitor your intake and change for the better. No question about that. Remember those daily diaries and accounts that the grandparents kept, which tracked how much they spent on tomatoes (four annas?) and what a sari cost? Indians are used to keeping monthly accounts.

Humans quantify the big things through self-reflection. Benjamin Franklin, for instance, was famous for keeping track of personal virtues[2]—thirteen of them—in a journal so that he could change for the better, and push himself towards the moral perfection he so craved. In an unfinished record of his own life that he kept and which was published posthumously in 1791 under the name, *The Autobiography of Benjamin Franklin*,[3] the great inventor talked about how keeping a daily log helped him change. 'I was surprised to find myself so much fuller of faults than I had imagined, but I had the satisfaction of seeing them diminish.' Gandhi and Nehru also wrote journals and letters where they examined their moral compass (as well as the nation's direction) and reflected on ways to improve it. Today, we have devices that help us do this.

There is a surfeit of data flowing around the world today. It seems that you can keep track of everything you do from when you wake up to when you go to sleep. You can track how much you eat, the kind of foods that you are drawn to, the quality of the air that you breathe, and your emotional states—whether you are depressed or delirious—your insulin, cortisol and cholesterol levels; when you had your last asthma attack; your exercise performance; and everything in between.

Wearable devices such as the Fitbit help with this self-monitoring. Such activity is called by many names: life logging, self-tracking, bio hacking, auto analytics, self-quantifying, self-surveillance and of course, the quantified self. The extent to which people quantify themselves can cause you to roll your eyes in bemusement. But they work.

You could argue that it would be simpler to remember such things. However, research shows that relying on our memory to report what we eat and how much we exercise accurately leads to mistakes. Devices and data don't lie.

So, go ahead. If you have a smartphone, download a 'quantified self' app, and track what you do from waking to sleeping. You might surprise yourself, and change for the better. For the record, I tried this. Not only did I fail, but I also detested the process. I felt like a caged bird, having to monitor every second of every day. Worse, given that I can now do this passively, thanks to smart devices, I find I have an aversion to even looking at the quantified version of myself. On the other hand, my husband has made significant life changes thanks to quantifying himself in certain key areas. I guess it goes back to that old Greek dictum once inscribed in the forecourt of the Temple of Apollo in Delphi: Know thyself. Lastly, use tools that work for you.

41

Track Your Habits

THE OTHER DAY, I got an email from a bewildered friend. 'You keep talking about this quantified life, but what should I quantify?' she asked. Well, here is a list of apps that can measure every aspect of your life and body. Choose what you'd like to measure and have at it. Diet: There are several apps to help you keep track of what you eat and how many calories you intake per day. Walking: Pedometer apps that are fitted into your smartphone measure the 10,000 steps that we are supposed to take every day.

1. Exercise: Armbands like Fitbit and Jawbone UP24 continuously monitor how many steps you take every day your sleep cycles and your fitness levels.
2. Sleep: Do you have trouble sleeping? Sleep Cycle, Zero, WakeMateand Lark, smartwatches and rings, rank the quality of your sleep: how long you slept in the REM sleep cycle stage, how deep your sleep was and things like that.
3. Moods: Do you feel down? Do you know why? MoodKit, MoodPanda, Moodscope, MoodJam, Happiness, Track Your Happiness and other apps help you track your feelings and emotions through targeted questions such as, 'Are you feeling annoyed or threatened?' which can, at times, trigger your state of mind. But once you are invested in this, they also offer suggestions on how to improve mood.
4. Productivity: Productivity apps are huge and targeted just to make you feel efficient or be effective. For instance,

AskMeEvery allows you to input a specific question on their prompts, 'Every day, ask me' and 'by emailing me at'. This is open-ended to questions such as, 'Every day, ask me how much time I spend practising the piano?' It sends out an email with the same question to you every day. It is like a nagging mother, except that the app does this.

5. Drinking: Several apps, such as DrinkControl, Alcogram and AlcoDroid help people track their alcohol intake. They use games to help people figure out their coordination, reaction time or reflexes, memory and emotions to determine if the alcohol has impacted their brain.
6. Asthma attacks: They are horrible. Help at hand begins with AsthmaMD; Asthma Tracker helps asthmatics track when and where their attacks happen to figure out patterns and responses.
7. Short workouts: The 7-minutes Workout apps force you to work out for precisely seven minutes. There is no excuse not to do the jumping jacks, squats, wall-sits and abdominal crunches it makes you do. You cannot say, 'I have no time.'
8. Period cycles: In case you want to get pregnant.

If all these sound freaky ('Yikes! Invasion of privacy'), they are not. Quantifying and reporting personal data will be the wave of the future. Whether you embrace it or not depends on one fundamental question: do you have offline methods such as written to-do lists or journals to help you keep track of the things you want to? If so, ditch the apps. If you (like me) love anything new and enjoy apps and gizmos, by all means, go for it. Even if you are an early adopter of apps and gizmos, you may not buy into the meticulous details expected by the apps offering the quantified self. If so, create a version of it.

For me, the thing I am tracking—not with an app but using my memory, faulty as it is—is just: eye strain. Since I spend a large chunk of time on the computer, I am accustomed not to blink my eyes. By the day's end, they are dry and fatigued. So, these days, I close my eyes and consciously try to relax once a while.

42

Figure Out How You Walk and Work

HOW DO YOU WORK? If you are like many of the readers of this book, you probably spend long hours in front of a computer. I do. It didn't occur to me that the chair I was sitting on was the source of my back problems. It took me several visits to an orthopedic surgeon and an acupuncturist to realize that I had to change my work patterns, hence my proclamation that the second villain of the modern age is the simple chair.

Anthropologists say the human body is made for standing and walking, not sitting. We sit far too much and far too long. So, how do we incorporate standing and walking into our lives?

Some Silicon Valley executives work using an 'air desk', a stand that allows you to type on your laptop while walking or running on a treadmill. Many use standing desks, and others walk while talking on the phone. The late Apple chief executive, Steve Jobs, was famous for his walking meetings, where he would discuss business issues with co-workers while taking a walk.

Walking your way to health is a cliché. Everyone advocates it. In his 2011 book *Thinking, Fast and Slow*, Nobel-prize winner and economist Daniel Kahneman talks about the speed of walking. A stroll at your normal pace, he says, is good for mulling over or coming up with new ideas. In contrast, power walking at high speed requires effort and attention from the brain and body, leaving less room for the serendipity of brainwaves or brilliant ideas.

In his 2013 book, *Daily Rituals: How Artists Work*, author Mason Currey has surveyed the work habits of 161 writers, artists, philosophers, scientists, composers and other geniuses. Walking daily was a common habit for many, along with working early in the morning and not having a cluttered desk.

Charles Dickens walked for three hours every afternoon, as did Beethoven, who carried a sheet of paper in case a musical score struck him. Russian music composer Tchaikovsky timed his walks to two hours exactly, not a minute more or less. Philosopher Soren Kierkegaard came straight from his walk to his writing desk to feed his thoughts into words.

How often have we told each other to go out for a walk? Yet, how many of us busy professionals actually do it? I certainly don't, usually because I have emails to reply and tasks to finish. Knowing that a walk may make us more productive, might nudge us to put on our shoes and get out.

Where you walk also makes a difference. For example, if you walk out in the open, amidst nature, for about forty-five minutes, the benefits are far greater than if you walk on a treadmill for the same time. In a 2015 study titled 'The Benefits of Nature Experience: Improved Affect and Cognition',[1] an interdisciplinary team of environmentalists and psychologists led by Stanford professor Gregory N. Bratman randomly assigned two groups to take a fifty-minute walk.

One group walked in an urban environment, the other in a nature reserve. After the walk, the participants were given tests to study their mental states and cognitive functioning, and they did well on mental function tests. More interestingly, 'Compared to the urban walk, the nature walk resulted in affective benefits (decreased anxiety, rumination, and negative affect, and preservation of positive affect) as well as cognitive benefits (increased working memory performance),' the study observed. Being amidst nature is inherently calming. But when you walk outside for forty-five minutes, the brain literally regenerates itself. Other research has shown that new cells are created during long walks.

According to Frederick Gage of the Salk Institute, our minds and bodies associate long walks with primitive migrations when we had to move from one place to the next. New brain cells are created during such long walks, because we had to figure out the new environment and make sure that it was safe for inhabitation. In response, our brains created new cells to make sure that we were prepared for new dangers and exertions. Frederick Gage, by the way, was the co-discoverer of stem cells.[2]

The next time you hesitate to step out for a walk in the evening, or you grab your cellphone to listen to music or podcasts while walking, think again. Multitasking while walking might make you believe that you are productive, but it may make you oblivious to the real benefit of walking in solitude amidst nature. Doing so for at least forty-five minutes will invite the muse to sit on your shoulder and whisper ideas or solutions that may not have occurred to you during your busy day.

Indian pavements, where we have to keep track of whether there is a pothole or cow dung on the way, have an added advantage: it not only exercises your body, but your mind is also forced to stay alert.

43

Use Synchronicity for Creativity

A FUNNY THING HAPPENED when I needed to look up the meaning of a word recently. Instead of typing it online, I picked up two rusty books that were nearby—or rather, strategically placed there. One was the dictionary, and the other a book on the etymology of words (word origins). What happened was that I began with the meaning of the word 'perspicacious' and ended up scanning through a list of words nearby that sparked a new way to explain the concept. In other words, it was as if I had thrown up a series of balls, and they magically formed a constellation. Swiss psychologist Carl Jung coined the word, 'synchronicity', a way of viewing events that happen at the same time but are not causational, i.e., one doesn't lead to the other. For example, you think of a friend and the phone rings. Turns out it is the friend you were thinking about. This is synchronicity.

To game synchronicity is beyond the scope of this book and falls perhaps in the realm of magic. But there are things you can do to work with synchronicity in order to bolster creativity or idea generation. Using a dictionary to find new words leading to new ideas is one. Using your LinkedIn feed add to your task list another. Say you need to find a VC for your startup. You open LinkedIn, and a friend's article in which he is talking about a conference he has been to appears. Look up the conference and follow the breadcrumbs to see if it leads you to a VC. This requires a less goal-focused and more open-ended approach to thinking. Try it a few times and see if it works for you.

The humour writer David Sedaris uses this to extreme effect. I once stood in line to get an autograph. Before he signed, he asked each person in line a random question. Here is a sample list from my time on the line: When was the last time you got robbed? Did you dream of an earthquake yesterday? Have you ever had a pet snake? Coming up with these questions requires creativity, but the answers gave him gold for material for his writing, and yes, he has written about his process of asking his autograph-seekers random questions in some of his essays.

For a while, I tried a version of this. I started announcing to people at parties that my lifelong goal was to be a stand-up comic. It produced the desired effect. People laughed. If you saw me, you would know why. I don't look funny; I don't talk funny. In fact, I am pretty galactically unfunny. It feels pathetic to admit this, but announcing this desire to be a comic is my funniest line.

What happened next was more interesting. Certainly more than the small talk that happens at a party. Some people talked about their own deep and unfulfilled dreams. Others suggested nightclubs with open-mic nights. Still, others gave me jokes.

One man told me that the trick was to silence the voices in my head—that say I don't have a funny bone in my body and will, therefore, fall flat. The trick was to actually get out and engage. To act, to rush 'rashly' towards the goal instead of thinking over it once, then twice, and then putting off action for another week.

Near my home is a club that offers stand-up opportunities for amateurs every Thursday. I think that I need to get out there and attempt comedy. Next week, I aim to do just that. A quote I read while flipping TV channels said: 'Make sure that your worst enemy doesn't live between your two ears.'

I plan to use that bit of synchronicity to further my creative confidence.

44

Drink like the Chinese and Sweat into Your Suit

WHAT IS THE ONE thing ancient India and ancient China have in common? No, not martial arts, which originated in India and went to China with Buddhist monks. It's that both ancient Indians and Chinese drank hot water. No ice water for them, and this is as it should be.

When all else fails, hot water should be your go-to beverage. Carry a flask. Fill it with hot water; add lemon and honey, if you wish. Imbibe. This simple drink should serve as an alternative to iced drinks or soda with a meal.

The Chinese still do this—they drink hot tea. Ancient Indians did, but today, few of us do so. Ayurveda advocates hot water as an accompaniment to food. Even today, Ayurvedic spas in Kerala only serve hot water with meals.

A 2013 study titled 'The Effect of Water Temperature and Voluntary Drinking On The Post Rehydration Sweating'[1] says that hot water increases the amount of sweating, leading to a 'thermoregulatory response' in the body.

Digesting food requires your stomach to create enzymes and acids that break down the food. Ideally, you should not drink water with your meal and dilute these stomach acids. If you must drink, drink lukewarm water in small sips. Cold water is like dousing out a fire, which, incidentally, is how the ancients thought about the digestive process. Traditional Chinese medicine still uses the phrase 'stomach fire' to describe it.

Hot water has the bonus of breaking down the fats that come with the food. Now, this isn't fact, but it makes imaginary, and intuitive sense. It is possible to visualize this, even if you cannot prove it scientifically.

The takeaway? Drink lukewarm water in small quantities, if necessary during a meal. At all other times, drink hot water. It will make you sweat and improve your digestion. Speaking of sweat, go one step further: figure out how to sweat.

I can hear you say, or at least think, 'I am paying good money to get instructions on how to sweat?'

You exercise, and you sweat, right? Well, my friend, it is a little easier than that. I'm about to suggest a way of sweating without too much exercising. Wear a sweat suit. It is available in India. I heard about it in the US first. It is a big trend there to wear sweat suits while exercising. The website 'Kutting Weight' sells a line of 'sauna suits' that people wear while they jog or exercise so that they can sweat buckets rather than a mere stream.

The companies that sell sauna suits claim that wearing these heat-trapping clothes enhances the effects of exercise. They list out a bunch of dubious benefits, including detoxification, reduction of muscular damage and so on. It is similar to the logic of Bikram Yoga, where people do asanas in high temperatures.

Whether or not these suits offer all the benefits they claim to provide, one thing that all of us can do, without spending hundreds of dollars on exercise equipment, is dress warm while exercising. Sweating benefits exercise.

Counterintuitive as it seems, dress in layers rather than shorts when you go to the gym. If you end up sweating like a hog, you can console yourself by thinking that the benefits of losing all your water weight outweigh your sweaty woes.

45

Use Your Pinky for Your Smartphone

THIS IS ANOTHER WAY of saying, use your least-used body part. It could also apply to your senses—do you smell enough, not in body-odour but through your nose to sniff out smells sense? Babies come out with their eyes shut and noses open. The smell is an ancient reflex we give up once we become eye-focused. But you can regain by focusing on it.

Similarly with the pinky. As you may have guessed, this book is about getting you out of your comfort zone in a low-stakes everyday manner. One habit that all of us have developed is typing onto our cell phones, usually using the index finger. Using the pinky little finger will jostle that habit quite a bit, particularly if you use the pinky from your non-dominant hand. It will balance out your body parts and how you use them.

The same thing applies to mental models. All of us have certain favourites. Some tried-and-tested ones that we adhere to have become a second-habit. Some of these are mental models we have inherited. Buying things on sale may be something we have inherited from our parents, even though our circumstances may have changed enough that we can afford to buy what we want at full price. Don't get me wrong. I am not dissing frugality. I am only asking you to question your mental models. Or, for that matter, everything you hold dear and has become second nature.

Begin with your pinky. The next time you punch into your smartphone, use your non-dominant hand and pinky.

46

Become Aware of First Principles from the Kitchen

One of the prettiest women I know in Delhi quoted the titular phrase. She is seventy by years, and forty-five by looks. People often ask her husband if she is his second wife. When I asked her for beauty secrets, she said, 'use the kitchen counter'. Every day, as she makes breakfast for her family, she uses whatever is available to prepare a mask and apply it on her face. It could be tomato juice, potatoes, papaya, honey, lemon juice, oats, yoghurt, cucumber peels or a mixture. The point is to do it every day, even if it's applied only for fifteen minutes.

An underused but magical ingredient for beauty treatments is a plant that is indigenous to India: *Curcurma aromatica*, or kasturi manjal (junglee haldi) as it is called in our vernacular tongues. This wild ginger is anti-inflammatory, anti-bacterial, antioxidant and a whole range of 'anti' prefixes aimed at positive benefits. Indian women have used this plant both internally and externally for centuries. It staves off wrinkles, evens out the skin, fights acne and blackheads, and some believe it makes one look years younger.

Why has it fallen out of favour? I think that is because it is hard to procure and mix. In Chennai recently, I had to walk around Mylapore to discover the Naatu Marundhu Kadai or country medicine shops that carry *Curcurma aromatica*. You buy a little bit and mix it with other ingredients, such as rose petals, orange peels, and green moong dal—sold individually. Then, you walk to the nearest flour mill to grind the whole thing into a powder.

This powder is mixed with milk or water and applied every morning. Just listing these steps makes me tired. Why would a busy professional do all this when stuff in bottles is readily available, albeit at five times the price?

I don't have the discipline to mix masks every morning. But here's something that I have started doing. I grow brahmi, tulsi, betel and Indian borage (called karpuravalli in Tamil). Every so often, I walk out onto my balcony, break off a few leaves, wash them and pop the entire combination into my mouth. That's right. Take a variety of fresh leaves and throw them into your mouth. If possible, chew on this first thing in the morning. I started doing this to combat colds and improve my memory. Now, it has just become a habit.

The other plant that grows plentifully in Indian gardens is aloe vera. Walking around my building every morning, I take some aloe vera gel and apply it on my face. By the time I'm done walking, the sweat has washed off the gel.

Many people drink a concoction of lemon juice, paprika and honey, diluted with some warm water when they wake up—both to lose weight and improve the digestive system. If you don't have the patience to make this concoction every morning and can stand the sourness, simply cut half a lemon and chew it as I do. In that hilarious movie *Goodbye Girl* (1977), actor Richard Dreyfuss drives his girlfriend mad by chanting, 'My body is a temple, and therefore, what I put into the temple has to be holy.'

'Holy' is what we call prasad or prasadam in India. You don't have to go that far and eat only prasadam. An easier dictum to remember is: what you eat first thing in the morning is important. Don't screw it up or waste it by chugging down some soda or coffee. If possible, eat and apply healthy ingredients on your face and hair before you drink your morning coffee.

First principles, as we all know, matter.

47

Watch Birds and Animals

DO YOU HAVE A cherished image of yourself that is entirely delusional? I know: which one, right? My cherished image of myself is that I'm a naturalist, not just any old naturalist: a naturalist-healer. The kind that can not only identify every species of bird but also walk by a plant and say, 'This is a copper pod tree. Crush its seeds, swallow for ten days, and you will have a cure for your piles.'

The fact that I need to hang around people with piles to prove my prowess as a naturalist-healer is pathetic even for a dream. What is scarier is the distance between my dream image and reality. I once made a fantastic Pesto Genovese—with neem leaves. The taste of it still haunts my family. Plant identification is not my forté.

Recently, I decided I would become an expert on birds. I would start small, begin by observing the birds that populated my urban habitat. Once I had learnt their names and mating calls, I would learn about birds from all over India and then the world. In the diaphanous fairytale that was my dream, I would write a book, *Birds of Every Kind with Every Mating Call in Every Species in Every Corner of the Earth.* That was the plan anyway.

This attempt brings forward two contradictory impulses. One, which I call the habitat theory, suggests that things like bird watching and music are learnt young. People grow up with birds all around, and if they haven't taken the interest or effort to figure them out when they are young, there is little chance that they will as an adult.

The opposite theory is based on neuroplasticity—that you can learn anything at any age simply by setting your mind to it. For the purposes of my experiment, I chose to believe in the latter.

Armed with a pair of binoculars and a bottle of my favourite Indian red, I ventured into my balcony—and was promptly overwhelmed, not by the cacophony but by the camouflage of noises. Horns mooed in place of cows; a Coppersmith Barbet sounded like the dug-dug-dug of a construction machine which makes holes in the road; squirrels screeched like parrots; and dogs wailed like death was coming. Ten minutes later, I beat a hasty retreat.

The next morning was better, perhaps because I drank coffee instead of wine. Right away, I could identify three species of birds: parrots, crows and Brahmini kites. I ate some chocolate as a congratulation and continued looking. It was then that I encountered my first problem. You see, birds don't wait in one spot for you to identify them. They make these beautiful singing noises from somewhere within a large tree, and you cannot spot them. You can't even spot the exact tree inside which they are hiding.

After a few days of sweeping my binoculars back and forth like the flailing sails of a ship capsizing mid-sea, I happened upon a Millingtonia tree, called chameli in Hindi. It has one key virtue: it is tall and has white flowers as a contrast to the green all around. I trained my binoculars at the top of the Millingtonia and experienced my first victory, which led to my first concept note for my future book: if you are patient, you will notice that birds come to flowers. You don't need to chase them figuratively with binoculars.

Over the course of several days, things improved. Certain elements are key for a non-birdwatcher or a nouveau birdwatcher like me. Limit bird watching to fifteen minutes, but do it every day, preferably early in the morning or at dusk.

Try your best to capture an 'aha' moment every day; a moment of joy; a source of pleasure. For me, this came when I was training my binoculars at a distant tree as usual, and happened to discover a Kingfisher sitting quietly on a branch. At least, I think it was a Kingfisher because there was some blue on it.

This highlighted the next obstacle in bird watching: how would I know what I was looking at? Books helped, but I found that *Wikipedia* was my best resource. Try typing in 'Birds of Delhi' or 'Birds of

Bengaluru', and there is usually a helpful blog dedicated entirely to urban birds.

Using this Wiki page I identified the birds with the sweetest sounds as bulbuls. They have a little tuft on their head, and after listening to them carelessly singing one morning, I raced through the house, looking out through every window until I spotted them on top of a tree with giant red flowers. By typing in 'tree with giant red flowers in Bengaluru', I learned that this was the African tulip tree or *Spathodea campanulata*.

Mother nature has bestowed beauty on every species, but she has been exceptionally generous to birds. Watch a bird, any bird, soar in the sky, and I guarantee you will feel joy and envy. The freedom birds seem to experience is uplifting, and you wish you could lift yourself.

Here are some things I learned. Pigeons can fly great distances, and I find them to be the most efficient flyers. They streak through the sky, following the same rhythm, without veering off course, as though focused on a goal. Crows are whacko, particularly when flying in pairs. I have seen crows fly and then suddenly dip ten feet as if a wind current funneled them downward before lifting themselves back up. Parrots fly well, but not for long distances. As for the Brahminy kite (*Haliastur indus*), I am unsure if I like them.

What is the point of this? To engage with nature, improve my memory by memorizing species names, get fit by walking up and down spotting birds or reduce stress being surrounded by greenery.

Do you see that we are hitting all the points of this book? So, watch birds, bees, butterflies or spiders. It doesn't matter. Just get outside.

48

Wear Herbal Clothes

Of ALL THE NEW-AGE remedies littering the market, few would seem as seductive as wearing clothes to gain good health. But that is precisely what the Handloom Weavers Development Society in Kerala proclaims with their hand-woven herbal textiles. The clothes made of these herbal textiles are called Ayurvastra, and you can look these up online at Ayurvastra.in.

This non-profit society has over 600 members, mostly rural illiterate women, and is based in tiny Tumbbad village, an hour's drive away from Kerala's capital city, Trivandrum. The Handloom Weavers Development Society ships all over India, with an online shop on its website.

With swaying coconut and banana palms, rain-grooved red earth and verdant paddy fields, Thumbod used to be called the 'Manchester of Kerala' for its long tradition of weaving for the Travancore royal family, that died out with the advent of power looms.

A few years ago, two brothers who belonged to the weaving families hit upon the idea of using organic herbs to dye their hand-loomed textiles. Years ago when I interviewed them, they said that immunity levels are raised when using these medicinal textiles, and the body reaches a certain mental and physical equilibrium.

Today, a whole community of weavers uses old recipes for herbal dyes and sells these clothes online. The weavers use local medicinal plants to stain their yarn and dye their clothes. Pomegranate skin imparts pink; turmeric, yellow; indigo, blue; tamarind, brown; onion skin, light orange; and black plum, black.

The raw yarn is first soaked in cauldrons of organic bleach. After a few days, the yarn is coated with herbal gums extracted from banana sap, tea leaves, basil extract, guava skin and other gooey stuff. Finally, it is woven into fabric and soaked in herbal dyes that 'catch' on immediately thanks to the herbal gums.

The biggest beneficiaries are the woman weavers, who get paid a third more than market wages. Most women weavers work at home while looking after their families and children. These weavers have sought out tribal women in nearby hill stations to see if the hill tribes can grow medicinal plants and herbs, many of which are endangered.

As consumers, we may not have access to such potent medicinal plants, but we can buy these weaves online with just a click and stitch them into clothes that look good and, if the claims are valid, improve our health.

49

Cultivate Tiny Habits

IN HIS BOOK, *THE Power of Habit: Why We Do What We Do, and How to Change*, author Charles Duhigg interviews a US Army major based in Iraq. As Duhigg notes, the US military (or any military) is based on habit formation. It teaches soldiers how to think, shoot and communicate under fire.[1]

The army major states that understanding habits is the most important thing he has learnt: 'You want to fall asleep fast and wake up feeling good? Pay attention to your night-time patterns and what you automatically do when you get up. You want to make running easy? Create triggers to make it a habit.'

Every year, we make resolutions—lose weight, get fit, exercise more, diet, be more productive, stop procrastinating, stop wasting time on social media, get a new job. This year, quite late in life, it occurred to me that habit-formation is the key to making any goal a success. I used to think that if you wanted something enough, you would work to achieve it. During the long days of dogged effort in pursuit of a marathon or mere weight loss (although that isn't a small goal), one needs strength to persevere.

The word effort comes from the Old French word 'esforz', which means power, strength and force. Certain simple habits can offer this kind of strength. The trick is to figure out how to make them your own.

One way is to trick the mind. This is what successful practitioners, in Walter Mischel's famous 1970 'Stanford marshmallow experiment' did. His subjects were four-year-old children. Those overseeing the experiment left the children alone in a room with a marshmallow and said that if they didn't eat it, they would get two when they returned.

As has been widely documented, the children who succeeded in staying away from the marshmallows used distraction as a device. They sang to themselves, curled up on the floor and played imaginary games, and tried everything to distract their minds from that sweet wonder just a few feet from them.

The same can apply to adults. When you want to avoid that late-night snack, offer your mind appealing distractions that are on par with a treat. Watch a favourite show, solve puzzles, read a gripping book, do anything feel-good and absorbing.

Next, figure out your mental triggers—what causes you to reach for that extra doughnut you don't need? What makes you grab that packet of chips? What makes you drink another can of Pepsi? Once you figure out these thought triggers, you can work on eliminating them.

As I said in an earlier chapter, Stanford professor B.J. Fogg wrote a book called *Tiny Habits: The Small Changes That Change Everything*, in which he suggests the 'If This Then That (IFTT) approach'. Some of his suggestions are: I will do one push-up every time I use the restroom. Now, this doesn't work in offices in India, but maybe you can incorporate a version of this: after I pee, I will stretch is a good one.

Whatever you wish for this week, year or decade, make it a habit. A tiny one.

50

Sing

BEFORE WE SPOKE, WE sang. As a species, we wailed with sorrow and hooted with laughter before we could express our feelings through words. The question then becomes: how much do we wail, sing, or even hum these days? This isn't about singing as a performance. It is about singing as an expression. Singing when we walk down the stairs. Humming while waiting for a cab.

Try it. I know that I sound like one of those meditation classes, but not only will it soothe and elevate your spirits, it could make you work better as well.

Much chatter has recently linked success with performance art, music and dance. The logic is that working with creative teams, be it in an orchestra or dance troupe, is great for your professional development, even if you aren't a musician.

In her talks and articles, author Joanne Lipman, author of *Strings Attached: One Tough Teacher and the Gift of Great Expectations*, suggests that music is the key to success.[1] Quoting sources as varied as Microsoft co-founder Paul Allen, filmmaker Steven Spielberg and former US Federal Reserve chief Alan Greenspan, the author makes the case that music helps achievers process things better in all aspects of life.

When you play the violin in an orchestra or dance as part of a company, you have to pay attention to both visual and musical cues. Music allows us to see patterns, learn to time and think in rhythm, all of which are necessary in various fields, including managing people (looking for visual cues) and in most creative areas.

I know what you are thinking. You are not a musician. But you don't need to be Yo-Yo Ma, Lata Mangeshkar or Kishore Kumar to enjoy the benefit of this skill. You can sing in your shower, on the stairs or just to get out of your head. I sing because music connects me to aspects of myself that I cannot even fathom, let alone understand. It brings forth images in my head, unbidden and unasked, images that may lead to an idea for an essay or speech. Music relaxes me and forces me to be in the moment. Most importantly, it links me to a culture that is part of my identity. It pleases me to be singing the same song that was sung 400 years ago. Occasionally, my music surprises me.

I began learning music in Chennai, which is the bastion of Carnatic music, the classical form that originated in south India. The city transforms into a hotbed for music lovers from December to February. They come from far and wide to listen to daily music concerts given by the country's top artists. This is the 'Chennai Music Season'.

On some really bad days, when I sing a classical piece (to myself) particularly badly, I ask myself why I sing anything classical at all. Instead of berating myself for faltering during some difficult musical phrases, wouldn't it be better to be a listener? Why do I still sing? Well, about my music, I am hugely self-critical and obsessive, so I keep practising. Music reveals the deepest parts of myself to me: the parts I don't accept or like.

Holding up this mirror also shows me how I must change.

51

Overlearn

EVERYONE—FROM ACTORS MEMORIZING SCRIPTS to musicians practising new songs, to teachers helping students understand facts—knows that learning takes time to settle in the brain. Research shows that if you learn something new and then quickly learn something similar right after, the second thing you learn can get in the way and make it harder to remember or master the first one.

The way to solve this? Overlearning. It explains why musicians and dancers keep practising a movement after they have perfected it.

A 2017 study published in the paper *Nature Neuroscience* suggests that 'Overlearning hyperstabilizes a skill by rapidly making neurochemical processing inhibitory-dominant'.[1]

In plain English, this means that when you learn something new, learning it beyond the plateau stage will stabilize and bind it into your mind. Yes, you could argue that with AI, you don't need to learn anything because ChatGPT comes to the rescue. But there are still things that AI cannot do for you, and this has to do with your passions: AI cannot make a great meal, memorize the words of a song, figure out how to handle a camera, dance a sequence, swim the backstroke, hit a ball right to the mid-wicket, or pass the basketball or … need I say more?

'Overlearning' or repetitive practice, has far-reaching implications in any field of creative and physical endeavour, such as tennis, acrobatics or classical Indian dance. When we learn a new physical movement or dance form, the brain develops a 'sensorimotor map' that gets refined with repetition.

The new task triggers initially different neural networks and muscle clusters, but with practice, the body learns to eliminate the movements that deplete mental and physical energy until we perfect the move. But perfection, according to the study, is not enough.

The best students overlearn or continue to practise even after. During this phase, students who had already learnt the task would feel that nothing was happening, but this was the phase when the body digested the learned skill.

In other words, when the learner thinks they are doing rote movements, be it a tennis serve or a dance rhythm, their mind may believe that nothing is happening, but their body records a reduction in energy. This is called overlearning, and is key for a performer to go from good to great.

During this overlearning phase, when the body operates on cruise control, the mind and its intuition kick in and initiate tiny changes that make a performance sing. Moreover, since the body's energy is freed up for other things, it will allow athletes and performers to focus on other things, like anticipating the opponent's tennis move, playing the violin with more passion, or holding a dance pose for a moment longer to stay in tune with the live orchestra or musicians.

This is intuition and grace. It kicks in when you overlearn your movements, and this is particularly true in the case of sports or performance, which is all about emotion and timing.

Overlearning isn't an option for anyone who wants to succeed or excel in any field. It is *the* way forward.

52

Cultivate Open Attention

THIS PHRASE IS JUST a fancy way of saying: allow for boredom.

In his 2013 book *Focus: The Hidden Ingredient of Excellence*, author Daniel Goleman discusses the different kinds of attention.[1] The most obvious type of focus, he says, is concentration, where the mind is rooted in a task until a solution is reached. This type of focus is best suited to analytical work. Creative insights, on the other hand, occur when the mind is loose, open and aware. The history of science is replete with such instances.[2] August Kekulé described the structure of benzene 'when his thoughts were elsewhere,' as stated in John Read's 1995 book, *From Alchemy to Chemistry*. In it, and countless articles, Kekulé talks about how he worked feverishly to figure out the structure of benzene and when he stared at the fire, almost dozing off, the image of a snake eating its own tail (ouroboros) came to his mind and in a flash, he applied it to the structure of benzene.

Now, you may not be working on world-changing problems, although, let's be honest here, we all think we are, right? We are all legends in our own minds. Well then, how do you create legendary works in the arts, sciences or, for that matter, startups?

There are a few ways to trigger pathways that open insight and imagination. The easiest way is to go to sleep. As mentioned in a previous chapter, we often wake up and discover that the solution to the knotty problem we have been wrestling with has come to us overnight.

Another way is to meditate. Meditating, or accepting thoughts as they come and sending them on their way, allows the mind to relax. It expands and opens the brain and primes its receptors to ideas and insights that leap across boundaries.

I am a failed meditator. I tried sitting cross-legged and attempted to 'watch my thoughts', but sadly, they were all over the place. They did not make sense, and worst of all, they were mundane, tackling the kind of trivia that is traditionally the realm of children and old women: 'Should I have acted differently at the party?', 'Did I pay the right amount for those dozen apples, or did I overpay?', 'Did I forget to turn the gas off before ducking out the door?'

The third method is what I describe here. Consciously allow for boredom. Let the mind be idle. Today, we have to be productively employed all the time. When we iron clothes, we listen to podcasts. When we take a walk, we speak on the phone. When was the last time you did nothing? You ought to allow for boredom. When you go down the lift to get into the taxi, resist the urge to whip out your phone. Let the mind roam. You may be surprised about where it takes you.

53

Make Castor Oil Your Friend

GROWING UP IN CHENNAI, my mother used to recount a weekend ritual with distaste. As always, it was mixed with a lesson: 'You may think my cooking is boring and long for noodles, which you are not going to get, but at least you didn't have to go through the castor oil weekend ritual.'

Turns out that once in a fortnight, she and her siblings were lined up early in the morning and given a spoon of castor oil on an empty stomach. The result: a day-long rendezvous with the toilet.

'It was a reboot to our digestive system; it took out all the toxins,' said Mom. Around lunchtime, they were given kanji, a simple gruel of rice to settle their stomachs.

Today, on social media, beauty influencers talk about using castor oil for hair growth and moisturizing the skin. One technique is mixing castor oil with rose essential oil, applying it on your face before your morning walk and then washing it off.

My mother applied castor oil on the undersides of her feet during Chennai's summers. It cools you down, she said. When our eyes got dry, she would apply a drop of castor oil on our closed eyes and massage them. These days, I apply castor oil on my navel and put a rudraksh on top (don't ask me why: I just made it up because of my links with seed therapy and the learning that you need to trust your intuition about what works for you). I tamp down the rudraksh with some tape and go to bed. It helps me sleep.

Castor oil exemplifies the word unctuous. It smells vile. But if you can tolerate it, it has many benefits. Its use as a laxative goes back to the

Ebers Papyrus,[1] a papyrus of medical and herbal knowledge that dates back to 1550 BCE. In it, castor oil is recommended for hair growth.

The Brits, by the way, used castor oil to humiliate their servants. Those who forgot instructions were fed castor oil, according to the 2011 book, *Food Culture in Colonial Asia: A Taste of Empire* by Cecilia Leong-Salobir. Read it if you want your stomach to churn with anger.

Back to the plant belonging to the genus *Ricinus*—it grows everywhere in India and its oil is excellent for hair, skin and digestion. Use it.

54

Discover the Pleasures of Denial

I AM WRITING THIS as I face laddus, barfis, badam chocolates and mixture. The festive season is in full swing. It is a time for celebration, family and pain. People obsess over feasting and fasting. The eternal question that accompanies most happy events, whether weddings, parties or holidays, is: how can you enjoy the array of goodies that tempt the palate at every corner without putting on a few pounds?

It is this conundrum that I'm contemplating as I walk up the hill in Kashmir with a few fellow hikers. We have just finished a fantastic Wazwan or Kashmiri feast, replete with delicacies: kebabs, a variety of roasted meats and vegetarian dishes for me. I follow a fairly standard routine in such situations. I eat, replay the wonderful dishes I have just finished eating and dream about the food to follow. It is this activity that I'm engaging in when my companion tells me about a concept that is completely alien to my disposition.

I listen, mouth agape, as S.S. Bijral, a retired inspector general of police (IG) in Kashmir, tells me about the 'pleasures of denial'. In his red turban, IG Bijral cuts a spry, energetic figure as we walk up the hill. The Dal Lake sprawls to one side in the distance, and dense foliage hugs us in the other. I am doing the walking version of the 'stomach-pulled-in' manoeuvre that men do when they pose for a photograph. My mouth is open to avoid huffing and puffing, and I am trying not to show the dignified retired officer that I can barely keep up with him.

There are a few benefits of getting old, but for the life of me, I cannot remember them. Losing your memory and becoming acquainted with pain are undoubtedly two of the downsides to ageing. But being older also allows us the opportunity to impart wisdom to the next generation—and it is precisely this that IG Bijral is doing.

He says that finding pleasure in denial is a nifty concept, and one that he has been following for most of his adult life. The basic idea is whenever you find food and drink, both tempting and avoidable, figure out a way to deny yourself that temptation. We all know, temptation lurks in every corner. The dark chocolate that winks at you every time you open the fridge, the fifth cup of fantastic coffee that makes a case for the goodness of caffeine, the aromatic steak that is calling your name or that street food that reminds you of home.

All of these are wonderful and completely unnecessary. So, I ask him how he finds pleasure in saying no to these delicacies. The trick, he says, is to fast-forward into the future. Remember what happened the last time you drank that fifth cup of coffee; the sleepless night that resulted. Every time you see a piece of luscious red meat, imagine visiting the cardiologist and reading your blood test results.

'I eat until 75 per cent of my stomach is full and imagine how light I will feel later as I watch my companions continuing to eat even when they don't need to,' he tells me sensibly. 'I imagine them suffering from heartburn and bloating and me being as light as a butterfly.'

Put this way, it has a, shall we say, 75 per cent chance of success—at least in my case.

55

Find a New Way to Look at Traffic Jams

IN HER INFLUENTIAL BOOK, *Mindfulness*, Harvard psychologist Ellen J. Langer says that mindfulness is to make a concerted effort to notice something new in every situation.[1] When you go back home and meet your spouse, try to see five new things in them. That is a brave goal. What if you don't want to see new things in your spouse?

We Indians have a far more laid-back approach. Patanjali's *Yoga Sutras* instruct us to sit with our back straight and allow our minds to focus on one point. The Sanskrit word for this is 'dharana' or concentration, which leads to 'dhyana' or deep meditation.

Of late, Western researchers have used meditation techniques to improve the performance of not just monks and mere mortals but also soldiers and athletes. Take psychologist Amishi Jha of the University of Miami's Department of Psychology and director of Contemplative Neuroscience for the Mindfulness Research and Practice Initiative (yes, you can study these things in American colleges).[2]

Jha studies attention, working memory and how to improve resilience in high-stress situations. She has received funding from the US Department of Defense and the US Army to figure out how mindfulness training can help army troops improve their resilience and reactions to high-stress situations, to develop a mental armour, as it were.

Her lab gives US soldiers training in mindfulness so that they can cultivate discernment: a potent word in Indian philosophy and what we call 'vivekam' in Sanskrit. Mindfulness trains soldiers to be present and take control of the moment so that their actions don't result in 'psychological injury' to themselves or others, said Jha when I interviewed her years ago.

One mindfulness method that I've tried is modified staring. It is called trataka or trataka yoga kriya. A simple way of doing it is by 'candle gazing' (although this phrase does not do it justice). Trataka is about focusing your eyes on a particular object. It could be the flame of a candle, or your shoulder (there is a form of trataka that guides you to meditate whilst looking sideways).

There are four types of tratakas. Dakshina jatru trataka is when your head remains facing the front, but your gaze is focused on your right shoulder. Try it. The effect is that of a dancer who faces the audience, but her gaze is to the right. Vama jatru trataka is the same practice, except that the gaze is focused on the tip of the left shoulder. Namikagra trataka is when the gaze is focused on the tip of the nose. Bhrumadhya trataka is when the gaze is focused on the spot between the two eyebrows.

Another method is when you sit at arm's length from a candle placed in a spot where the flame does not flicker. The goal is to stare at the tip of the candle without blinking your eyes. Typically, your eyes begin watering after a few minutes. Then you shut your eyes and relax. Next, you bring a closed-eye gaze to the spot between the eyebrows.

These yogic exercises—that make you stare at your shoulders or the point of the third eye instead of at your smartphone—can reduce eye strain and calm you down.

56

Observe the Pain

I HAVE BEEN TRYING to figure out how to live with pain. Athletes do it all the time; dealing with sports injuries and pain is part of their lives. When the rest of us run a marathon, we begin with a few miles, then some more. We reach a point where our knees beg us to stop, but we keep going. That's how we make it to the finish line.

Since pain is part of the game, I decided I wanted to reorient my mind to view pain as something that would benefit, to give pain a positive spin. That way, when I experienced pain, my mind would not think of it as the end of the world. Instead, I would view it much like I view broccoli or karela (bitter gourd): something that I eat to eat ras malai or ice cream thereafter. Pain, inevitably becomes a preamble to pleasure.

My route to experiencing pain has been through martial arts. On a trip to Japan, I enrolled in martial arts classes. I chose Aikido because it looked easy. Kyoto has a sensei (a teacher) named Yoko Okamoto who does amazing things. Look her up on YouTube. She throws around men who are twice her size, whirls and twirls her way through multiple incoming attackers and emerges successful. I became interested in Aikido because it offer exercise and meditation benefits. It had the grace of dance and the added benefit of self-preservation.

I also found Aikido was suited to women because it involves taking the force and momentum of the attacker and turning it back on them. It is unlike Sumo wrestling, where you have to lift a 150-kilogramme man over your head and throw him on the ground. It is not even like boxing, where you use your muscular strength to punch your opponent senselessly. It doesn't require tools like sticks and swords. All Aikido requires is a nimble body and a centred mind.

After two hours of training, I discovered muscles where there ought to have been chakras or nerves.

It was galling when the instructor said: 'Enjoy the pain.' I felt like slapping her. She must've read my thoughts in my murderous eyes because she said, 'Go on; do it.' I rose to punch her only to find myself whirled into a somersault and flat on the floor: a cushioned floor, thank goodness.

When martial arts instructors say, 'Enjoy the pain,' they are talking about endurance. They want students to learn to tolerate higher and higher levels of pain and become mentally and physically stronger. Engaging in martial arts also allows me to trick my mind into believing that pain is a good thing because if you are in pain, it means that you have exercised or stretched yourself.

These days, I have a new goal. Every day, at least one part of my body has to be in pain. In other words, achieving pain is my goal.

I tried this approach when I first stopped going to the gym. If you are like me—somewhat sedentary—you don't need to do too much in order to experience pain. Lift your arms above your head and stretch sideways. Hold for fifteen seconds if you can. That will cause pain; at least, it did for me. What exercise coaches will tell you at this point—when you are wheezing and feeling unknown parts of your body—is that you have to get past that moment of pain.

Not really. Pain can become the goal if your hamstrings are pulling, your knees are hurting, or your back is aching, it means you have to pay attention to that area.

Long-term, once you trick your brain into thinking that pain is good, it will help you face the inevitable increase in aches as you get older. If you are lucky enough to be healthy and exercising, then tell yourself that you are going to be in pain every day. That is the goal, not the consequence. If you are in pain because of a medical condition, then none of these mind games apply. You just need to go and see a doctor.

To be in pain means that you are alive. Enjoy the pain, as my martial arts teacher said.

Of course, this doesn't work when you get a pain you didn't deserve or want—something like adhesive capsulitis or frozen shoulder that arrive out of nowhere. You didn't do anything to get this shoulder frozen. You were in fact, going to the gym. In such a situation, along with pharmacology, physiotherapy and regular doctor visits, you can try closing your eyes and paying attention to your pain for several minutes. Is the pain occasional or consistent? Does the pain move across areas or stay in place? Is it a pulsing, shooting or spread-out pain?

As the book *Confronting Chronic Pain* says, 'Pain begins as a physical reaction to a stimulus, but its interpretation by the mind is cloaked with an individual's feelings, experiences and expectations.'[1] The book lists the full spectrum of pain management, including prayer, Ayurveda and, of course, mindful breathing. My basic takeaway after reading this and other books dealing with chronic pain were to try everything—physiotherapy, pharmacology, manipulation under anaesthesia—but also include acceptance of the pain and, if possible, a measure of peace or relaxation with it. You don't have a choice with the pain, but like with everything else, how you deal with it is a choice.

57

Turn Your Enemy into a Friend

GIVEN THE CIVILIZED URBAN environments that most of us live in, you would think that martial arts would be redundant. It is not as if we walk on the streets deflecting attacks every day, like knights and samurais of yore. And yet, the world is obsessed with martial arts. They are thriving, with new ones being created every year.

The women of my building are learning Krav Maga, created for the Israeli Defence Forces (IDF). Krav Maga uses everything available, including vessels, nails, sticks and the odd piece of furniture for self-defence, not to throw at spouses.

I also engage in martial arts these days, mostly while lying on the couch. I love watching martial arts movies, preferably with a bag of bhujia sev.

I prefer watching martial arts movies to fashion shows. Somehow, the heroes of martial arts seem accessible—unlike the long-limbed supermodels with their sunken cheeks and sultry eyes. Models require good genes. Martial arts is a skill that can be learnt. Or so I'd like to think. When watching Michelle Yeoh in *Crouching Tiger Hidden Dragon,* I can almost deceive myself into believing that, with enough practice, I can run up buildings like her. Of course, that is not true, as my frequent yet chastening encounters with learning martial arts prove.

If you have discovered that standing upside down in yoga is not for you or that you cannot jump to thumping aerobic music, martial arts may be just the ticket to your fitness nirvana. This is particularly true if you are a disciplined person who enjoys routine. Everyone should attempt one form of martial arts at least once in their life. It could be

Kalaripayattu from Kerala, which is the mother of most Asian martial arts, Tai Chi with its focus on breathing, or Jujitsu. The training and mental focus will be good for you.

Although most people associate the martial arts with Asia, the etymology of the word hints at its European origins. 'Martial' stems from Mars, the god of war in Greek mythology. Europeans, like the natives of other continents, quickly devised instruments like swords and shields that would help them attack. However, Asian armies fought not only with weapons but also with martial art forms that gave them mastery in close-range combat and using pressure points in the body to maim and kill.

I don't maim and kill. I'd like to think it is because I don't have the killer instinct, but that's not true. Most martial arts are not about killing. Aikido, for example, has the lofty, compassionate goal of self-protection without injuring the attacker. One master said that the goal was to make your attacker your friend.

'But what if you wanted to attack your friends?' I asked.

The master's shining, wise eyes looked puzzled. 'I have never encountered this question,' he replied.

The Tao of War. Enjoy the Pain. Make your enemy your friend. Hurt people with compassion. It all seems very contradictory. But these are the nimble philosophies of martial arts. They make your body and, more importantly, your mind, agile.

They also teach you an essential skill when you get older—one that will prevent fractured hips and torn ligaments. Read on.

58

Fall

MOST MARTIAL ARTS CLASSES begin with stretches and so do mine. It was the tumbling that was difficult. Although you may think that martial arts is about fighting, it is also about falling—or, rather, learning to take a fall. As I tumbled and fell, I realized that falling is difficult and that falling without getting hurt is almost impossible. That falling is inevitable, and how you fall, which is mostly about reflexes, makes a difference.

It occurred to me then that learning how to take a fall, quite literally, would be a useful skill to cultivate, particularly as I got older. Martial arts classes do this as a matter of course, but there are other techniques, too. All they require is a yoga mat and a willingness to fall.

Here's a thought, weird as it may sound: why don't you tumble into bed? Remember how we used to do this as children and how much fun it was? Rediscovering the joys of doing a simple somersault is a great way to nudge yourself into falling.

The other method is to do those 'trust' exercises that some find terrifying: stand back-to-back with a partner, spouse or friend. Interlink your arms. Asked them to gently lean forward and take the weight of your body on theirs. If possible, lift your feet off the ground so that you are arched back, and your body is on your back. They control your body in a sense.

Losing control is the first step towards learning how to fall. Orchestrated falling is the first step to preventing injuries. And, preventing injuries is key to ageing well.

Functional trainers recommend a simple but arduous exercise. Stand on one foot. Lift the other off the shoulder, but above all do this with your eyes closed. The idea is to get your feet reflexes working again so that when you stumble (usually on one foot), the other foot reflexively knows how to respond. I have been doing this when I wear my earrings (two-in-one is the core of this book, anyhow). I can't last more than ten seconds in that. Try it.

59

Cultivate Your Intuition

BEFORE HE CO-FOUNDED APPLE, Steve Jobs spent seven months in India, an experience detailed in his 2011 biography. In it, Jobs gives his insights into the difference between intellect and intuition. 'The people in the Indian countryside do not use their intellect like we do,' he said. 'They use their intuition instead, and their intuition is far more developed than in the rest of the world. Intuition is a very powerful thing, more powerful than intellect in my opinion.'[1]

Jobs was not a fan of India. If he identified intuition as the one Indian thing that he wanted to emulate, that is worth considering. There are a few Sanskrit words for intuition, 'pratibha' and 'buddhimati' being two. Developing intuition, discernment (or viveka) and wisdom (vijnana) have been Indian preoccupations for centuries.

Different cultures are obsessed with different things at various stages of evolution. Japan, for instance, is obsessed with refinement and perfectionism. Singapore is obsessed with systems. China, with scale. The US, with innovation. Ancient Indians were obsessed with self-cultivation; to figure out how God thinks, to paraphrase Einstein.

In 1925, Einstein shared his guiding principle with a young student, Esther Salaman, 'I want to know how God created this world. I'm not interested in this or that phenomenon, in the spectrum of this or that element. I want to know His thoughts; the rest are just details.'

In a 1976 book, *The Metaphoric Mind: A Celebration of Creative Consciousness* by Bob Samples, the author paraphrases Einstein's view on metaphors, intuition and the sacred. In a quote attributed to him, Einstein said, 'The intuitive mind is a sacred gift and the rational mind is a faithful servant. We have created a society that honours the servant and has forgotten the gift.'[2] Notice that this scientist used the word 'sacred'—proving that the rational and the intuitive are not as disconnected as we make them out to be.

Intuition is something that every religion knows about. Jesus—as the story of Lazarus (and the fish with a four-drachma coin in its mouth) illustrates—was a man of intuition. As was Prophet Muhammad. In today's world, we call these intuitive thinkers visionaries. Religion teaches us that the way to develop intuition is through prayer and meditation. As Jobs says in the same book by Walter Isaacson: 'If you just sit and observe, you will see how restless your mind is. If you try to comment, it will only make it worse. But over time, it does calm down, and when it does, there is room to hear more subtle things—that is when your intuition starts to blossom.'[3]

Flashes of insight that are the result of intuition can occur when you awaken from the mists of sleep. This is the time when the free-flowing, loose, flexible stillness of the mind gives rise to solutions that are fully formed. During the day, the mind is a wandering beast. When you try to sit still and meditate, the mind wanders to knotty problems that need to be solved: who said what to whom and how to resolve unfinished business. But if you can still your mind and keep it loose, you increase the chances of insight, of the Muse sitting on your shoulder and allowing your imagination to flourish.

Ancient India was known for its approach to spirituality and the self. Today's India can jumpstart its innovation by focusing on creativity and imagination among its workforce—by allowing the mind to wander mindfully, to see the world in a little boy's open mouth, to activate the third eye, to sit still and follow the mind on all its various tangents and trajectories, to 'sniff the winds' like Jobs did, and sense what lies ahead.

60

Wear Anklets

As you can tell, I am obsessed with meditation, probably because of a contradiction. On the one hand, I fervently believe that it will solve many, if not all, my mental problems. All the anxieties and neuroses that I have, I think, will vanish if only I could still my mind. And here lies the great chasm. Meditation is the hardest thing that I have attempted. It is also the thing that I haven't cracked. I am so far away from succeeding that I would say that I am not even at the starting point. So, I try hacks and shortcuts.

Focusing on the moment is the gift that prayer and meditation afford. There are many things that civilizations use to centre their mind. Tibetans use bells. Aldous Huxley's 1962 novel, *Island*, recreates a utopian land, where parrots fly over people screeching, 'Here and now, boys. Here and now.'[1] They remind the islanders to focus on the present, to live in the here and now.

The anklets that Indian women wear serve a similar purpose. Their rhythmic jingle as the women walk brings to mind the musical sound, to the here and now. Try wearing them. This ability to voluntarily bring back a wandering mind again is called 'meditation'.

William James, often identified as the father of American Psychology, wrote the magisterial two-volume Principles of Psychology in 1890, which I haven't read, even though as an undergraduate student of psychology, I was asked to. But a quote from James from that book resonates with this chapter.

'The faculty of voluntarily bringing back a wandering attention, over and over again, is the very root of judgment, character, and will,' said James.

Seriously? Judgement, character and will are all linked to focus? That's a lot. This means that I have none, which stings to even think about.

The wandering mind is also the root of imagination and creativity, in my defence, even though I know that what James is saying and what I am saying are two sides of the same coin. Paradoxically, the controlled kind of wandering elicits the best results. Think of a kite—its string roots it to the earth and yet it bobs in the sky. That is the kind of mind wandering that we need to create.

A famous July 1985 cover of *Time* magazine featured Hollywood director Steven Spielberg saying, 'I dream for a living.'[2] Daydreaming creates the kind of associations that lead to blockbuster movies and companies, I might add. The trick, then, is to allow the mind to fly and figure out how to rein it in. Indians have numerous tools for this—the anklets, for example.

Neuroscientists ask people to close their eyes to see how much the mind flits around. When the eyes move behind closed lids, so does the mind. Bharatanatyam has a famous saying that is taught to every novice dancer. It is from the text *Abhinaya Darpana* (The Mirror of Gesture), written by the redoubtable Nandikeshvara. He was often said to rival Bharata Muni, who composed the *Natya Shastra*, the foundation of dance and other arts. In verses (sutras) 36–37 of *Abhinaya Darpana*, the author talks about focusing the mind and creating rasa or emotion. This famous verse goes, '*Yatho hastha thatho drishti. Yatho drishti thatho manah*. (Where the hands go, the eyes will follow. Where the eyes go, the mind will follow).'

Do you want to stay in the here and now? Breathe. And wear anklets. Even if you are a man. Why not, bro? We live in a metrosexual world.

61

Make Friends with Your Pineal Gland

IT BEGAN A LOW rumble several years ago when one of my daughters turned five. Many friends with teenage children commented on how their daughters seemed to attain puberty earlier than they had. While my generation started menstruating between the ages of twelve and fourteen, today's girls were hitting puberty at ten and eleven, they said.

When I expressed concern about this to my paediatrician, she suggested I switch to organic foods. Although there was no hard scientific proof, she said that the increased level of hormones in milk and meats probably played a role in the early onset of puberty.

I assumed I could do nothing about it for my two girls. After all, most foods are pumped full of growth hormones to make them appear plumper and larger. When children eat these foods, their bodies are affected. I figured that there was little a mother could do. Nevertheless, I switched to organic milk and forgot about it.

Later, I came across a method that seemed to counteract the early onset of menstruation actively. It had its roots in the Bihar School of Yoga—that emphasizes seva (service), asanas (yoga poses) and pranayama (breathing techniques).

What had me seeking out BSY was not my interest in yoga but my concerns as a parent. In a BSY newsletter,[1] Swami Satyananda, one of the school's founders, offered what seemed to me the most lucid description of how yoga could help children: teach them Surya Namaskar (the sun salutation yoga poses), basic pranayama, and initiate them into a mantra (a sacred word or phrase chanted over and over).

Doing this would delay puberty by two or three years, according to the Swami. Usually, puberty takes place between twelve and fourteen, and is established between fourteen and sixteen, but if the child practises yoga, puberty will start at fourteen and be established at eighteen.[2]

His explanation for this delayed onset of puberty also made sense. It had to do with the pineal gland, a little-known endocrine gland revered among yogis for being the seat of the third eye or the Ajna Chakra. I had paid little attention to this tiny spot, buried behind the centre of the forehead, caught up as I was with my earthly plight. I had no desire or time to 'open my third eye'.

Indeed, I spent most of my time shutting my two open eyes to the chaos at home. Now, it seemed, this little gland held the keys to preserving my daughters' childhood. If awakening the pineal gland could delay the onset of menstruation, I was all for it.

The link between the pineal gland is not yogic hocus-pocus but rooted in science. As any basic science textbook will tell you, the pineal gland is a pea-sized organ located between the two hemispheres in the centre of the brain. It has two main functions: to produce melatonin and to affect sexual development. In children, the pineal gland produces large amounts of melatonin, which, in turn, inhibits sexual development.

Conversely, when the sexual hormones progesterone and oestrogen kick in, the pineal gland calcifies and reduces production of melatonin. Most adults have reduced amounts of melatonin and a calcified pineal gland. The trick then, according to the BSY and numerous like-minded researchers, is to prolong the life of the pineal gland and increase the amount of melatonin in a child's body.

Simple enough, but how does one do it?

According to BSY, the pineal gland starts decaying once sexual impulses surface (and they surface earlier and earlier these days thanks to explicitly sexual movies and culture, not to mention hormone-saturated foods). In BSY, great care is taken to keep the pineal gland healthy for as long as possible; as long as the pineal gland is functioning, the release of sexual hormones will be kept at bay.

An Australian yogi taught me the techniques that would preserve the pineal gland. Philip Stevens, also known as Swami Samnyasananda'[3] is a practising yogi and, best of all, a parent. Stevens (or Swami Stevens as I began calling him) has conducted extensive research on the 'electrophysiological correlates of yoga breathing techniques'.

In other words, he studies how certain yogic practices can help heal our bodies. His area of interest is how certain techniques regulate the production of melatonin. Like the BSY, Stevens also believes that doing the Surya Namaskar, alternate-nostril breathing and candle-gazing helps increase the amount of melatonin in the bodies of children and adults.

The simplest technique Swami Stevens taught me was trataka meditation, also known as candle-gazing. 'Trataka meditation, using a candle flame to focus the eyes, can produce significantly higher levels of melatonin,' he said. Like all yogic techniques, it takes some doing, especially with children, because it involves sitting still. In trataka, you stare unblinkingly at a candle till your eyes water.

When I began this practice years ago, I would get my daughters to do it before their bedtime. Swami Stevens told me that he lets his daughters lie in bed and gaze at the candle, which helps them calm down and doze off to sleep.Yoga texts prescribe that the candle should be at eye level and at arm's length. If you have a young daughter and you are worried about an early onset of menstruation, you can do candle gazing with her on the bed. Ask your daughter to stare at the flame without blinking. Then, start counting from one to sixty. Halfway through the count, it is likely that your child will interrupt with cries of, 'It's boring. I want to sleep.' Let her lie down and tell her to gaze at the candle anyway; soon, she will drift off.

The other technique that helps melatonin production is alternate nostril breathing. My nine-year-old used to do this in tandem with candle-gazing at least for two rounds. Doing something instead of simply staring at a candle helped her retain her focus on the exercise. If you are able to, get your kids to do alternate nostril breathing while candle-gazing as well. I am not saying it is easy but teaching them this practice will help them in their lives ahead.

Alternate-nostril breathing is simple. Your thumb closes your right nostril as you breathe in through your left nostril. Then, your ring finger closes your left nostril as you breathe through the open right nostril. Breathe in through the right nostril and out through the left. Breathe in through the left and out through the right. And so it goes.

Most kids will not protest against the Surya Namaskar or sun salutation, a series of backward-and forward-bending poses that work while breathing. This is active and not 'boring' for them. It regulates the entire endocrine system and has the added benefit of energizing the body. Since it's more active than breathing or candle-gazing, kids enjoy it more. It's best to learn the sun salutation from a qualified yoga teacher and then teach it to your children. The endocrine system will be kept in good health by combining sun salutation, trataka and alternate-nostril breathing.

As Swami Satyananda says, these three practices will help 'preserve childhood'. If done regularly, yoga texts claim a delayed puberty—and therein lies the problem. Today's kids are so busy, and their lives are so hectic that it is difficult to find time for these yoga techniques. They don't take long, to be sure, but they require commitment.

62

Fail Well

I HAVE TRIED WATER skiing three times in my life. The first time was in Michigan, where a friend who lived on the river took some of us summer campers out on his boat. I was abysmal at it. I couldn't even stand up. The water rushed towards my face as the boat sped up. Breathless and gurgling with frustration, I tried to yank myself up on the skis and failed within three seconds, tumbling into the water. My humiliation was made worse because all my friends seemed to pick up this skill within a couple of tries.

The second time I tried it was in Goa. This time, I took a class, but the same thing happened. My instructors yelled from the speeding boat while I tried to balance on my haunches, holding the rope tightly. Again, within a few seconds, the rope slipped from my grip, and I sank into the water.

On a recent trip to Sri Lanka, I tried water-skiing again. This time, I was able to stand up. The joy that erupted in my chest, the sheer, undeniable sense of achievement, was intoxicating. Best of all, I had earned it. What do you do when you fail? Do you give up on that skill or activity altogether? That is the usual approach. But one alternative is to give yourself three chances before quitting. There is an added benefit if you are a parent trying to get your kids to take up a new skill or sport. The trick for any parent is to help their child find such experiences—where they may fail at first but then, after a struggle, succeed. That, more than anything, leads to self-worth.

63

Avoid the Fatigue That Comes from 'Task-Switching'

As I WRITE THESE words, I am sipping honey tea, trying to memorize the verse of a Carnatic music song by playing it continuously in the background and watching whether the cleaner in the next room is swabbing my red oxide floor with coconut oil as instructed. There is nothing special in that—we all multitask. Some of our tasks are supremely mundane, like my list above.

Other people's tasks are more meaningful. I would go so far as to say that a politician's task list during his entire life would never have included words like red oxide flooring or coconut oil. His multitasking would have to do with moving markets with a single phone call, and talking to Presidents while fending off the press, all of which would probably happen when I argued with my cleaner about the merits of coconut oil.

Recently, however, I have been looking at studies that question the whole notion of multitasking. The jargon that this research uses (switch-cost, task-switching) brings to mind an electric bulb, and one should immediately say, 'Don't multitask.' The 2022 study, 'The Location Independence of Learned Attentional Flexibility' shows that 'task-switching', which is when your brain moves from one task to another, has a 'switch cost'.[1] In summary, studies in cognitive psychology suggest that true simultaneous multitasking is unlikely. Instead, our brains are 'switching between tasks rather than handling them concurrently. This rapid switching between tasks has a cost: cognitive efficiency diminishes as the brain needs time to refocus each time it switches'.[2]

The point of all these studies is to show that multitasking is not as effective as we think it is. Every task requires a certain mental process and when we keep switching between tasks, it is sort of like a stop-and-go jerks of a car when it is driven by a beginner.

While multitasking, our brain never really cruises with the comfort that comes from engaging in only one task. This switch-cost increases if the tasks are complex ones. In other words, flipping the bird while driving a car is a no-brainer; but negotiating a complex deal while driving, really taxes your mental coefficient. Far better to pull over.

Most of us in today's world multitask constantly. We type SMS messages into our phone while we dine with friends; we talk on the phone while watching TV, which we do while reading *The Economist* in the first place. We read reports while going down the airport escalator and reply to emails while waiting in queues. Recently, I began thinking, do we multitask because we have too much to do, or because, as Cyril Northcote Parkinson said in his Parkinson's Law: 'work expands to fill the time available'.[3]

One Bengali friend told me that we all work to escape the terror of what Victor Frankl called 'existential vacuum'[4] in his classic 1948 book, *Man's Search for Meaning*. He had me depressed for the rest of the day. I didn't engage in a single task, let alone multitask. I engaged with my existential vacuum to prove him wrong.

I doubt that any of us can stop multitasking, but there are a few simple strategies to defray or reduce it. These are small things, but they can cause a paradigm shift in your thinking, like realizing that you can dunk your samosa in tea and it won't disintegrate. Some of you probably use all these strategies, but I would wager more than others.

Reduce the time you spend per phone call. Most of us multitask while on the phone. We call someone for a reason and get caught in a web of inane niceties that go nowhere.

If you are in the middle of something that involves extensive use of grey cells, don't answer the phone. Instead, pile up all your calls and call people back on your own time. Similarly, switch off your email browser for an hour and answer all emails in one shot.

Focus on the job at hand—oldest advice there is. Everyone from Zen monks to Uzbeki grandmothers say this. But it is hard to do. When I sit down before my computer, for instance, I am fraught with deadlines and work that needs to be finished. What do I do? I surf the Internet, read old emails, chuckle a bit, deride all the forwarders who send me idiotic emails about life on Mars, and I flame a few people. By the time I get down to the task, an hour has passed.

Figure out a way to write short but meaningful emails. This is deeply individual, but I think a good goal would be to keep every email to two sentences. Okay, speaking as one who writes in paragraphs, maybe to five lines. I have a friend who sends emails in which the message is in the subject line, and the email is empty. Try that. 'You guys coming to dinner today?' says the subject line. Nuff said.

Learn from the auto industry. Assembly lines are superb examples of doing one task after another.

There is one time, however, when you must multitask. As soon as spousal battles get underway, that's the time to declare you have to return calls or fold the laundry.

64

Organize Your Time

IT BEGAN INNOCENTLY ENOUGH and took a fairly standard trajectory. Prodded by stray comments from my spouse, a sibling, a friend and a parent, I virtuously decided to make yet another effort to organize my time.

As always, I began with grandiose plans that had no chance of being implemented. I would not begin my day by checking my email; I would instead hug a child, the spouse or at least a stuffed animal. I wouldn't lie in a somnolent stupor in front of the television, scarfing down chips while promising myself that each would be the last; I would ban potato chips from entering my household.

I wouldn't enter the shower and then realize that every single plastic bottle that littered the shower stall was empty. I would stock each bathroom with a host of fragrant products that would satisfy every human need, and then some.

I wouldn't go to the grocery store for just one (forgotten) ingredient or item at the last minute (this was pre quick commerce, by the way), just before the guests arrived for dinner and the cake was in danger of collapsing. I would, instead, buy several fridge magnets, make a running list of grocery needs starting every Monday and tack it onto the fridge, along with every how-to note. Then, on Sunday, I would shop (either online or at the stores) at furious speed for the week's needs. And so it went, my messy life.

In desperation, I turned to mobile applications that would help me. 'Efficiency apps,' I typed into my computer. Almost like magic, many websites, apps and advice columns popped up. There was one called 'iProcrastinate' that pretty much described my working process and helped me prevent it. There were apps like 'Pocket' and 'Evernote' that allowed me to clip anything I chose from websites into folders for future reference.

This was a vast improvement from my current system, which was to mindlessly scribble quotable quotes and flashes of insight on the first available paper and then go around the house in a state of permanent irritation, asking, 'Has anyone seen that discarded envelope on which I had written a line from Maya Angelou's poem? It was a yellow piece of junk mail stating that I had won the lottery and written "Phenomenal Woman" in one corner. Has anyone seen it?'

How do you manage the minutiae of your life and keep them from tipping over? Are you a clipper of articles, a list maker, or someone who uses an app with names like 'Clear' or 'Wunderlist' to get things done?

My method has been fairly simple. I prioritize the things I need to keep track of: flashes of genius, irreplaceable insights and the store's phone number that supplies school uniforms. Everything else falls through the cracks. I am in the market, if you will, for a personal assistant who will keep things in order.

Failing that, I have resorted to reading advice columns from scarily efficient people like Martha Stewart—who devil their eggs, glaze their pudding, iron their underwear, and tuck the corners of their bed linen into severe straight lines. They all begin with one piece of advice—actually two.

The first (to achieve household order) is to actually believe it is possible; that a permanent state of chaos and searching for objects is an aberration, not the norm. The second is to view such an outcome with admiration, not scorn. The latter seems to be my Waterloo. Cleanliness may be next to Godliness, but not in my book. If the universe began with chaos, chaos is good enough for me. This attitude may make me feel superior to all those busy worker bees who tirelessly file, scrub, segregate and organize, but it doesn't help in real life. I must emulate them rather than mock their ways. I must join the bees instead of thinking of myself above it all. Who am I—a queen bee? Even queen bees self-destruct without the colony.

As I write this, my desk is pristine; my newspapers are filed in an ornamental fashion; my fridge is full of magnets with important notes. Now, if only I could find that piece of paper on which I wrote the time for the doctor's appointment.

65

Drop Lists, Choose Pleasure

IN THE SPIRIT OF presenting both sides of an argument, I present below the opposite of the previous approach—the one I just wrote about in the last chapter.

Summer is a good time to examine life, so I did with mine. It was about time. I owed it to friends and family who had been nagging me to change my bad habits for years. Heck, I owed it to myself. I would manage my time better; I would stop procrastinating and get on that diet; write the novel I had been dreaming about, and open that restaurant. I would, as David Allen's book exhorts, Get Things Done—GTD to aficionados and addicts.

A sense of malaise, combined with a hankering for change, is a deadly combination. It manifests itself in ways big and small. You scour the local library for self-help books with cheery titles that manage to challenge and inspire (and these are made-up titles, by the way, so don't search for these books). *Eternal Optimism without clouds, End Codependency Permanently or At Least Today*. You start exercising and doing yogic headstands if possible. You force yourself to take long, calming breaths, ignoring that your diaphragm is constricting because of all that mental pressure. You start making lists.

Worst of all, you read lists, or articles with lists in them. You know the kind: 'Ten ways to make your life more productive'; 'Nine habits to ditch if you want to squeeze the most from the first hour of the day'; 'Twelve mistakes that losers who don't get things done, are doing'; 'How to be the top performer at work in ten days or less'; and, the final straw, 'Thirty-six things to do if you want to get away from making to-do lists'. I mean, is the irony not lost on these people? And yes, I get it. This book is an ode to that irony. A book with a list of 108 Ways in which a chapter rants about lists? You can roll your eyes now. Or stop rolling them. Back to the topic at hand.

Such lists are proliferating like turtle's eggs all over the Internet. Fun fact: Olive Ridley turtles come to Odisha's shores, and I have witnessed this 'arribada', as it is called, lay an average of 100 eggs per clutch, although the Ocean Sunfish (Mola mola) lays some 300 million eggs at a time, and the Male Seahorse which is the incubator of babies lays some 2,000 eggs at a time.[1]

But as someone who reads self-help books and essays with feverish dedication, I can tell you what hooks me. Some headlines are straightforward and follow the military dictum of saying it quickly and concisely: 'End Email Addiction Now,' or 'Throw away that time-wasting device'. Others do it more artfully by suggesting the opposite as if they know the thoughts in your head: 'When your mind says, "I can't", know that you can'—a typical headline that is best faced after a double shot of caffeine, which as it happens, is good for you according to the latest research.

In theory, I was the target audience for such lists. After all, I didn't merely bookmark them to read at a later date (which never usually came). I actually read them. My friends were a great help in this regard. They were all gainfully employed or ran profitable businesses and were busier than me. Their life was built around big words—maximizing and incentivizing productivity and efficiency—while mine was built around improvising. They were, quixotically, my source of self-help articles, even though they seemed to be doing great without any help whatsoever.

When I let it drop that I was—once again—in the market for self-improvement, my friends began forwarding me essays and lists with gusto. I dutifully read them. They gave me a halo effect for some time and made me feel that I could actually implement the suggestions.

It took several months and nearly 20,000 such forwards before I realized I was diligently reading and deleting everything without doing a darn thing. I wasn't changing a single behaviour or even a thought process. Thanks to all those lists, I was merely feeling myself in the throes of change. It was like continuing to eat ice cream while watching aerobic exercises on TV. You felt fit without doing the work.

Rather than do the work, I chose a novel approach to address the problem (that is entirely in keeping with the theme of this book). I began questioning the whole premise of such articles. I questioned the assumption that increased productivity was a worthy goal. The more I thought this way, the faster I realized that productivity was overrated. The whole point of becoming more productive was that you could get a lot more work done. For what and to what end? To be a bum on the beach? You know how that story goes, don't you? If not, look it up.

66

Get into the Zone

I HAVE ALWAYS BEEN a hardworking sort of gal—and no, this is not a preamble to some irony-laced witty statement. Sadly, it is what it is. A combination of a middle-class Indian upbringing compounded by the Puritan work ethic of the north-east US, where I went to college, has made me into a worker bee and occasional drone. The fact that I am not efficient about it is why all my efforts go to naught. But still, it must be said: I am diligent. This is all very well if you want to work, but not so great if you want to spur your creative juices.

There are several activities that get people into what is sometimes called 'the zone', where the mind empties and thoughts flow. In his book, aptly titled *Flow*, positive psychologist Mihaly Csikszentmihalyi called this the 'flow' experience, but applied it more in the context of peak performance when a person was fully engaged in and energized by the task s/he was doing, whether it was rock climbing or painting.

A flow experience involves losing yourself in an activity that is usually solitary. Shopping with a friend, in other words, doesn't count, there is too much nattering about price comparisons and coupons.

Unlike *Flow*, the zone I am talking about involves a certain disengagement from the task at hand, a trance-like state in which creative thoughts pour in, new ideas appear and problems get solved. Musicians call this being in the groove. The monks who discovered some of the finest things in life, such as coffee and beer, did this while being in the prayerful zone. Some people experience this while showering; others while running, speed-walking, listening to a concert, or even washing the dishes. You can be active or inactive to get into the zone, although physical activity offers a two-for-one experience: good for the body and the mind.

Zone activities are those that you approach willingly, and they usually leave you refreshed and less tired than you were when you started. Scrubbing the bathroom floor might take a saintly few steps to the zone, but for most people, the zone is reached through pleasurable physical or mental activity: birdwatching, singing, skipping. Children do this naturally. The trick is to sustain it as an adult.

Once you get to a certain age, you realize three sobering things: you are no Einstein; all those teenage aspirations that you had about changing the world will come to naught. And I cannot remember the third reason, which is probably reason enough in and of itself. An unexamined life notwithstanding, nothing most of us do will matter beyond a span of, say, two days or ten.

How, then, do you reframe your life? You choose pleasure. You cultivate hobbies. You imitate children. You fritter away time in meaningless but absorbing activities. Anyone who has or watches children will realize this. I don't buy those psychology books that state that babies use a lot of heavy-duty brainpower when they lunge, jump, gurgle and coo. That's a sorry attempt to justify fun as work.

Regardless, productivity is for the bees. Life is more than productivity. It is also about stopping to smell the jasmine wherever and whenever you feel like it; and not having to schedule time for it. It is not about unplugging one day a week, just so you can rewire your brains to become productive the next day. Life is not a script with a beginning, middle and end. Well, it is, but that sentence just sounded good. Sometimes, life is not about analyzing or achieving. Let me just say this: productivity is overrated. Choose pleasure. And if you make a T-shirt out of this slogan, remember to give me some royalties.

67

Figure Out Your Shoulds

HERE'S WHAT I WOULD like you to do. Insert the question 'Really?' after each of the below sentences.

People should be polite. Families should be comfortable saying things to each other on WhatsApp or other family groups.

Siblings should speak to each other every day.

Bosses should be fair to all employees.

Love is not having to say sorry.

Indian homes have no closed doors.

Each of the above sentences is what I call a should. A worldview that you hold dearly as the gospel truth. A worldview that you don't question.

Here is the problem: shoulds close you off because of a simple truth. Not everyone thinks like you. Not everyone has the same should that you do. And not everyone cares for your shoulds. In fact, they may resent it. As a parent, I told my kids a long list of shoulds. Indian homes have no closed doors was one, told usually with a cultural halo shining around my head. The problem is that once my kids went to college and were used to closed doors, they didn't like this should. They resented and rebelled against it.

To stay open, to keep people close to you, to earn the respect of your colleagues involves two things: the ability to listen and see things from another person's point of view and the humility to admit that your way is not the only way.

So, lose the shoulds from your life and see the ripple effect it has on your relationships.

68

Use Lessons from the Church, Mosque or Temple

WHETHER OR NOT YOU are religious, activities done in religious places can be incorporated into your daily routine in healthy ways. For instance, you can kneel and bow into a shashankasana (child pose) for a wonderful back stretch.

Prostrating yourself before the gods (the south Indian namaskaram) is a great exercise as you have to squat, bend, stretch your back and rise up again. It involves multiple muscle groups. Do this about thirty times for a great cardiovascular activity.

Personally, my favourite is what south Indians call thoppu karanam. To do this, cross your arms and hold your ear lobes while doing deep squats. As children, we were taught to do this in front of Lord Ganesh, but I find that doing it while standing in a cubicle also works.

It became famous for a while when a YouTube video proclaimed that doing this activity would increase your IQ. Why do you think Indian kids are so good in Math, asked the video. It is because of this age-old practice of massaging and pulling your earlobes while you do squats.

Whether or not this is true, religion offers great scope for exercise. Many south Indian temples are high up on a hill, and you have to climb some 200 steps to get to the sanctum sanctorum. While you're there, you circle the deity several times, prostrate to it, and sit cross-legged on a hard floor. All of these are great. The same thing applies to a church or mosque. You kneel, bow and walk.

Since this book is not only about the physical, let me also emphasize the mental and spiritual. I believe that all religions offer a path to divinity. Studies show that faith and spirituality give great emotional strength in times of crisis and goals. A.R. Rahman prays before composing every song and look at what he has accomplished. Communicating with the divine by visiting religious places or incorporating prayerful acts into your life, offers strength and solace.

My only hope vis-à-vis this book is that by the grace of God, may you prosper physically and mentally.

69

Look Up—Literally—and Look Inside

LOOKING UPWARD, BY THE way, is an under-rated exercise. If you simply stare up at the ceiling while in an elevator, it will help combat the screen-stare that we all do all day and every day and the shoulder bump that we all get due to it.

The classic time to do these short exercises is when you open a new page on your internet and the throbber spins. Yes, I learned that the spinning wheel which circles as you wait for your page to load is called a throbber. What do you do during this 'dead time' when the throbber spins? Most of us stare hard at it, willing the page to load.

Here's a thought: Do something else while waiting for the page to load. Shrug your shoulders, shudder, look away, close your eyes, look up, look at the distance, yawn, stretch the muscles in your face, wiggle your legs, shave a cat's head, if you want. All of this goes back to the original trigger: know thyself and what works for you, which brings me to the second part of this chapter: look inside.

Some years ago, I took a routine blood test and discovered that I had hypothyroidism, a condition in which the butterfly-shaped thyroid gland produces lower levels of the thyroid hormone. Typically, with hypothyroidism, you have to take medication for life, to substitute for the hormone depletion. I do that, but I have also decided to explore the holistic options I am naturally drawn to.

Even the most conservative allopathic physician will admit that endocrine disorders—more than other pathologies—respond to mind-body medicine. It makes sense. Anything that has to do with hormones, depression, memory and balance has a mind-body component to it. Anytime a doctor tells you that you have to reduce your 'stress' to get better, you might as well explore alternative remedies.

Stress is a nebulous thing—you can't see it; oftentimes, you cannot even feel it until it gets the better of you and leads you to a breakdown. Stilling the mind through yoga or meditation has been proven to help. With this in mind, I returned to one holistic field I have studied for years: traditional Chinese medicine or TCM.

Let me begin with the caveats: although I am deeply interested in holistic medicine and have practised various forms on myself, I am not a trained practitioner. The suggestions below are just suggestions, and must not be substituted for a visit to a qualified physician. My goal in writing this section has a simple takeaway: ultimately, people must take charge of their health.

You consider all options, consult experts and decide what works for you. For all their good intentions, allopathic and alternative medicine, in general, operate within silos. They don't talk to each other. It is up to us to find the doctor who is proficient in both practices. The other option is considering alternative therapies.

Read on to know the ones I have been exploring.

70

Try Other Systems

BEFORE THERE WAS MEDICINE in the version that we know now, there were healers and shamans. Before there were double-blind peer-reviewed studies, there were amulets, talismans and healing concoctions given by midwives, mothers, village elders and priests to the sick. Don't get me wrong, I am not taking away from the incredible advances that science has made. Without modern medicine, our life spans would be shorter and our health poorer. Today, however, there is allopathic medicine, and at the other end of the spectrum are alternative methods. The two don't meet or talk to each other. It is an either-or system. A question that is increasingly being asked is: why can't it be also-and? Why can't we take metformin for our diabetes, and at the same time, use Biodynamic Craniosacral Therapy (BCST) for our nervous system?

In 2011, Harvard created the Program in Placebo Studies & Therapeutic Encounter (PiPS).[1] It remains based at the Beth Israel Deaconess Medical Center in Boston. Its director, Ted J. Kaptchuk, studied Chinese medicine and wrote the seminal book, *The Web that Has No Weaver*, published in 1983, on that topic. In 'The Power of Nothing',[2] a 2011 profile of him, published in *The New Yorker*, he said that 'an important component of medicine…involves suggestion, ritual, and belief'.

Rigorously researched books such as 'Cure: A Journey into the Science of the Mind Over Body',[3] published in 2016 take that argument further and talks about how the mind aligns with the body to heal. As Dr Kaptchuk told *The New Yorker*, 'We need to stop pretending that it's all about molecular biology. Serious illnesses are affected by aesthetics, by art, and by the moral questions that are negotiated by practitioners and patients.' All ways of saying that prayer, mantras and talismans all help.

Now that I have attempted to convince you of my ways, here are some things that I follow, try and practise on myself and my family.

There is Ayurveda, but there is also Reiki, Chinese medicine, Hoponoponopo, BCST, Pranic healing and Bach flower remedies. Don't give up your doctor; complement your health with complementary medicine. Consider mind-body systems starting with yoga and going on to traditional Chinese medicine or TCM.

Traditional Chinese medicine, perhaps more than any other system, connects the mind and body—inside and outside—in a way that is both pragmatic and profoundly philosophical.

One option I follow is acupuncture, mostly because I am familiar with it. In my twenties, I interned with an acupuncturist, Eileen Karn, a thriving practice in Stamford, Connecticut, for about three years. Every day, I assisted her in the office and learned treatment protocols from her. I followed her around as she saw patients and needled her—literally, not metaphorically (well, maybe metaphorically too)—on weekends. Acupuncture considers mental and emotional components as important as the physical, both in terms of disease and healing. Kaptchuk, a trained TCM practitioner, is testing the mind-body balance as director of Harvard Medical School's Program in Placebo Studies, a remarkable programme that every physician would do well to get acquainted with.

Chinese medicine takes a composite approach and views organs as having a mental component. The kidney, for example, is thought to be the seat of will-power in Chinese medicine. If you want to strengthen your will-power to get a task done—run a marathon. Chinese acupuncturists, for example, will work on the kidney meridian. Similarly, one reason for sadness or depression could be the stagnation of liver qi (chi).

An oft-recommended herbal powder for depression is 'Xiao Yao San', which means 'free and easy rambler or wanderer' in Chinese. The Chinese word for deep sadness, 'yu', is also used for stagnation. In TCM forums and mailing lists, a protocol often recommended for depression goes something like this: regulate liver qi, tonify spleen, nourish blood.

A site I visit frequently, www.acupuncturetoday.com, has a few protocols for hypothyroidism. Following my usual caveats and disclaimers, none of the points I've referred to or those that are mentioned on a website are a substitute for proper medical attention in case you have a medical condition. My suggestions have to do with improving wellness. I am not suggesting how to treat illness, nor am I qualified to.

Acupressure is a gentler form of acupuncture. You don't need needles to do this. All you need is knowledge of specific acupuncture points. You then press the points, either using the tip of a pen or pencil or just your index finger.

A few acupuncture points are considered powerful, and these are the ones I have been using in my self-healing sessions. One is called 'Stomach 36 (ST36)' or 'Zusanli' in Chinese. The ancient texts say that needling the Zusanli will make you live 100 years, and this acupuncture point is used for many ailments. The Zusanli point is easily found by placing the palm of your hand over your knee. The spot where your middle finger ends is this point. Pressing this point during the course of the day is rejuvenating.

Let us say that you are sitting at a boring meeting or that a guest is visiting your home. You are forced to sit in a place and converse with him. One spot you can massage is called 'Large Intestine 4' (LI 4 or 'Hegu' in Chinese medicine). In Chinese medicine, this is the point that influences the face and digestion. So gently press it while you chat about the latest movie or where to go for dinner. Important: This point is contra-indicated if you are pregnant.

Acupressure can be done at any time and at any place. For a busy working professional, that is its power.

While I turn to acupuncture, you can turn to whatever resonates with you. The point is to explore all options with an open mind. As a cancer survivor wrote in *The New York Times* in 2018, 'Talismans and amulets—objects believed to have magical powers—were once part of any self-respecting doctor's medicine bag.'[4]

71

That 10 p.m. Snack

HAS THIS HAPPENED TO you? It is late at night, and you are doing what you usually do—watching a game on TV, answering emails, reading a book or whatever. Next to you is a snack: some Indian namkeen—masala peanuts, potato chips or chanachur. You reach into it in a rhythm that is part-desire, part-desperation and mostly guilt. You have skipped dinner, announcing to everyone that you are on a diet. Now the household is in bed, and you are downing fistfuls of this spicy siren of a snack, every mouthful making a mockery of your diet and your statement. The worst part? This isn't the first time this has happened.

There is a theory that most of us regress to our roots in different ways. We may be English-speaking, wine-drinking, secular, cosmopolitan, globally travelled Indians. But in some aspects of our lives, we return to our childhood.

Bankers who have shed every vestige of their Indian past find themselves crooning to babies in their native Sindhi or Marathi. The Goan advertising executive who otherwise only savours the finest cigars and wine will take a secret swig of feni. The Lucknowi lady speaks no Urdu, save for swear words, and the Westernized Punjabi executive who specifically chose a stunning Brazilian model as a wife suddenly finds sari-clad women sexy.

For many of us, this regression has to do with food cravings, typically at midnight, when away from home. Even the CEO who has distanced himself from the caste, class, religion and region he was born into yearns for curd-rice or poshto when alone in a foreign hotel room.

As for me, I must have been Marwari or Gujarati in my previous birth. My cravings have little to do with the idli and dosa I grew up with, but mostly with farsan or bhujia.

The craving hits at 10 p.m. after everyone has gone to sleep. I start insouciantly, elegantly spooning handfuls of bhujia sev into a bowl, ostensibly to calm my hunger pangs. I finish the bowl and find I cannot stop. Namkeens are my guilty pleasure and dieting pitfall. Thenkozhal from Grand Sweets in Chennai, chaklis from Thom's Bakery in Bengaluru, khakra from Chheda Stores in Mumbai, jhal muri from Kolkata; I have them all in my snack cabinet.

I am a savoury person—though not an unsavoury character (sorry, couldn't resist). I can look a gulab jamun in the eye and turn away without flinching. Gajar halwa does nothing for me. Kerala's famed payasams are an afterthought. As for any sweet that has a coconut filling, I scorn them entirely, having grown up eating twenty years of barfis and purans. Only Kolkata's sweets stir some saliva in my mouth, but not sandesh. Too dry. I like my sweets gooey—like tiramisu and mousse. Kolkata's rasgullas come close. They are spongy and rich and, thankfully, not too sweet.

Savouries, on the other hand, are my—and I would argue, an Indian—weakness. I can polish off an entire table of them just while reading a book. I think one of India's great inventions is the notion of a savoury snack that is not bland, like a pretzel or cheese ball. Our namkeens are pungent, tart and spicy. Like dal moth, chanachur, cornflakes mixture and my personal favourite, bhujia sev.

When I was a kid growing up in Chennai, my mother would take us to Parry's Corner, to the Marwari stronghold. There, amidst the narrow bylanes with shops selling electrical coil and hanging lights, you could buy bhujia sev that was not pre-packaged but made fresh every day. My brother and I would mix the bhujia sev with thick yoghurt and eat it at night after dinner. It was divine and rationed out. I still crave namkeens at night, usually after a satisfying music concert or other satisfying activities.

For us vegetarians, namkeens are a great balancer. In my opinion, Gujarat and Rajasthan are namkeen havens. South India, too, has savouries, but they don't have that spicy kick. Our murukkus, omapodi and chaklis are all very nice, but spicy? They are not. Gujarat, in particular, with its penchant for farsan, would be a namkeen taster's paradise. Gujarati farsans are not chilli-hot, but the besan flour gives it an exotic flavour to my south Indian tastebuds.

I wonder if we Indians crave sweets or savouries. I would wager savouries. What do you eat or drink at night, after dinner, when alone? It may tell who you are, far better than a Myers-Briggs test can. As for you, figure out your 10 p.m. snack. And why you need it. And then, if you can resist this Waterloo of childhood temptation. Got a foolproof method? Share it with me.

72

Look at a Childhood Photo Album before a Snack

MOST WELLNESS EXPERTS SAY that we eat for various reasons, and surprisingly, many of them don't have anything to do with hunger. Sometimes we eat because we are bored, or because we are lonely, or because we are stressed out and tired, or because we long for comfort.

The trick is to figure out why we are reaching for that tub of ice cream. Is it because the ice cream reminds us of a happy childhood memory? If so, we would be better served by opening up the family album and looking at old photographs while sipping some water.

All of this sounds great but there is only one problem: no matter what we do to it, water will never taste as good as ice cream.

73

Don't Phub Your Spouse, Practise the Pomodoro Instead

PHUBBING IS IGNORING THE person with you in favour of your phone. And just how many times have we done that—in public, furtively and with apologies ('I just need to check this message, sorry').

In my case, the penny dropped after a lovely family get-together. Instead of laughing, mocking and taking apart the party, like we used to do, the four of us—my husband, me and the kids—got into the elevator, whipped out our cell phones in unison and began tapping and swiping. It was ridiculous. According to the latest jargon, we were 'phubbing' each other.

The word is a portmanteau of phone and snubbing. I have to admit that I am a phoneaholic. It is my go-to device for comfort with Instagram for boredom, Facebook for connection, WhatsApp groups for intimacy and Notes to ensure my productivity. I have forty-three apps, each of which guarantees a dopamine hit (a feel-good hormone), and many of which I rarely use. But, like fenugreek in the kitchen, it is good to have all the apps there.

I have five birding apps, four meditation apps, multiple fitness apps, which have all failed to motivate me, an Indian Panchang calendar to figure out the full moon, a business card scanner called Haystack, which is very useful, and more games than I care to admit. I touch my phone more often than my spouse; I connect with family through it and seek it out like a secret lover every chance I get.

Like most folks addicted to their devices, I am often disgusted with my behaviour. 'I have to do a digital detox,' I tell myself. I make grand plans of switching off my phone at 7 p.m. to sit cross-legged in Buddhist nirvana, hoping that clear and present ideas flow into my head. I make these plans because my life has become a significant distraction; it gets in the way of my using my cell phone. A 2016 study published in the journal *Computers in Human Behavior* states that this holds good for most of us, at least the married populace.[1]

The study is on spousal satisfaction and I read it since I was seeking to improve mine. I don't know if it is the same in your marriage, but I bug my spouse to put his cell phone down (he doesn't bug me to do the same, but more on that later). I pretend I am doing it for his sake because it is good for him, like taking vitamins, but really, it is a call for attention. At least, that is what the study says.

'Partner phubbing (Pphubbing) can be best understood as the extent to which an individual uses or is distracted by his/her cell phone while in the company of his/her relationship partner,' the abstract states.

Don't we all do that? After all, what is the point of a spouse if you cannot take him/her for granted and choose the cell phone over them? But then comes the kicker. The study states that those with 'anxious attachment styles' report higher levels of cell phone-related conflict with their partner than those with less anxious attachment styles.

In other words, bugging my spouse to choose me over his phone means I have an anxious attachment style. My spouse has no problem when I am on the phone. He nags about other things—being punctual is his pet peeve—but he doesn't care if I use the cell phone, probably because he wants to be left in peace to use his.

But I? I see the cell phone as his mistress. Someone that my husband turns to in place of me. The ideal scenario would be if I could use my phone with impunity while he ceased all cell phone usage the minute I walked into the room. In other words, he wouldn't phub me.

What is the solution then?

One couple I know decided they would end each day by sitting together for fifteen minutes—without phones. The idea was that they would talk to each other about their day and connect with their feelings. 'The prospect is terrifying,' the husband confided to me. 'But hey, she wants it, so we are trying it.'

The experiment lasted two days, and guess who called it off? 'She,' phubbed her husband.

My solution is very novel. It is an app called Forest. I plant a tree in the app. It grows. If I pick up my phone, the tree dies. I can prescribe the time it will take for the tree to grow. For now, I am following the Pomodoro technique and have said that my tree will grow in twenty minutes. Twenty long minutes without checking my phone? I must be nuts. Or is this the road to sanity? I don't know. Worse, it's reached a point where I cannot differentiate.

I will keep you posted about my trees.

74

Work Easy Instead of Working Hard

I BEGAN SKIING AS an adult. Snow is hard to find in Tamil Nadu, where I grew up, hence the delayed start. A few lessons later, I was pronounced an intermediate skier. Mid-level ski instruction differs slightly from what I learned as a beginner. For the first time, I heard phrases such as, 'You have got to relax and trust the mountain.'

High up on a 'blue-level' (intermediate skier) slope in the Himalayas, my instructor, a ponytailed man named Hari, told me that my problem was that I was trying too hard and my muscles were too tense from the exertion of trying to learn. 'Relax,' he said. 'Don't work so hard.' It isn't easy to work less. It involves a mental leap of faith to go against years of conditioning.

When you are growing up, nobody tells you to 'work easy'. They all tell you to work hard. As contradictory as it may seem, in order to get better at sports like rollerblading, skiing or ice-skating, you have to work easy. You have to simulate the relaxed muscles of a child who has no fear and very little concern for achieving goals. To a child, skiing is just another new adventure in a vast unmapped life.

With an adult, as far as I can make out, trying a new adventure sport—be it rock or mountain climbing, windsurfing or bungee jumping—the body responds to new stimuli in three ways: fight, flight or, when you are stuck on a rock-cliff, freeze.

The Virtual Fear project at the Centre for Cognitive Neuroscience, *Duke University*, simulates a fear-filled 3D environment using virtual reality gadgets.[1] Fear-inducing memories cause panic attacks. The trick is to tame the flights of mind that imagine what could happen.

Focusing on improving specific skills—how to brake while skiing down a curved slope, how to pull yourself up to the next rock ledge—helps channel thoughts. The term used these days for this skill is mindfulness. Elite sports professionals use another term: trust. They demand you to visualize and trust that your ability to do it. Reach the next goal, climb the new mountain and work less hard at it.

Eventually, I did learn to work easy. I exhaled a lot; forced myself to relax; and did all the seemingly counterintuitive things that my instructors told me to: lean forward while skiing even though I was terrified I would fall on my face. To my surprise, it worked. The more I practised, the better I got.

Best of all, I could carry the work-easy lessons to other sports like rollerblading. The trick is to hold your body softly as if it were a young swaying branch, instead of a hard, firm tree. Children do this and animals are masters of this underperformance, which is actually peak performance.

I took to visiting aquariums to watch the fish. They spent much of their time in suspended animation, swaying with the ebb and flow of currents. They did not struggle to improve their posture or technique. They only did so much or rather, so little, in order to stay ahead of the game. Birds did the same thing, especially the eagles and hawks—they simply spread their wings to let the wind currents do the work. Every now and then, they flapped their wings to steer their course.

Gradually, I learned to ski like an animal. It involved an intense awareness of my body. Every time I felt myself tensing a muscle, I exhaled towards suppleness. I am still a rudimentary blue-slope skier, but slowly am slouching towards excellence by working less, not more.

75
Smell Stuff

PERFUMES ARE DEEPLY SYMBOLIC and perishable. Unlike a pashmina shawl or book, perfume does not last forever. Even if your great-aunt doesn't like the Amouage perfume you gifted her, there will come a time when the bottle is finished, and she can go back to the Damascus rose essential oil she uses.

Perfume has its roots in worship. The Latin root of the word, 'per fumum', means 'through the smoke'. Ancient cultures burnt fragrant resins, wood and incense as a way of purifying the space and making a plea to God. Most Eastern cultures light wicks, incense and wood sticks in prayer spaces. There is nothing like curling smoke to make a symbolic wish seem like a message to the heavens.

Ancient perfumes were stored in earthen vials or amphora later in specially crafted glass bottles, they were objects of beauty. Today, artisanal perfumers rue the mass-marketization of scent—international federations force perfume companies to test their products and remove any allergy-producing ingredients.

The traditional roots of perfumes—flowers, fruits, woods, resins, herbs and spices—are viewed as potential allergens, thus dissipating the joy for elite 'noses' as perfumers are called.

The good news is that there is a back-to-the-basics approach among elite perfumers. Rather than using thousands of synthetic ingredients, they are turning to the building blocks of traditional perfumes like ambergris, musk, jasmine and sandalwood.

The other trend in global perfumery is the use of fewer ingredients. In the past, European perfumes had hundreds, if not thousands, of ingredients. Now, niche perfumers are trying to use seven or eight.

The ingredient that has the perfume industry salivating these days is oud or frankincense. Demand for this resin is rising, with everyone from Tom Ford to Jo Malone adding oud to their fragrances. Most perfume houses use chemical duplicates to recreate the scent of oud, but some luxury perfumers prefer the raw ingredient. Real oud is both scarce and expensive. The best comes from Oman.

The Indian equivalent of oud is sandalwood—also a rare and scarce ingredient put on the government's protection list. In Bengaluru, sandalwood trees have to be reported to the local authorities and cannot be cut. They become state property. Mysore sandalwood is the best and forms the base of numerous male colognes.

In India, we use incense to perfume our spaces and oils to perfume our beings. Indian women use perfumed oil in their hair; in fact, a famous Tamil poem has a verse that talks about the heroine's scented hair. My favourite writing on perfume is not from ancient Tamil poetry. It comes from the late great Palestinian poet Mahmoud Darwish, who wrote about the sense of smell in his tour-de-force book, *In the Presence of Absence*:

> Cities are smells: Acre is the smell of iodine and spices. Haifa is the smell of pine and wrinkled sheets. Moscow is the smell of vodka on ice. Cairo is the smell of mango and ginger. Beirut is the smell of the sun, sea, smoke, and lemons. Paris is the smell of fresh bread, cheese, and derivations of enchantment. Damascus is the smell of jasmine and dried fruit. Tunis is the smell of night musk and salt. Rabat is the smell of henna, incense, and honey. A city that cannot be known by its smell is unreliable.[1]

In it, Darwish, who was facing imminent death, wrote about the scent of life and death:

> Exiles have a shared smell: the smell of longing for something else; a smell that resembles another smell. A panting, nostalgic smell that guides you, like a worn tourist map, to the smell of

the original place. A smell is a memory and a setting sun. Sunset, here, is beauty rebuking the stranger.

It is this evocative, nostalgic aspect of scents that perfumers aspire to transmit. The best perfumes can remind you of your father, or a particular holiday, or a city. The scent of pesto can take you to Italy. That of salted water can take you to Greece. Great perfumes affix the mind to a specific place and time, which is perhaps why we love them.

India, along with Arabia, contains the apex of scents. Our people know how to use scents. So said respected French perfumer Serge Lutens when I met him in Paris for an interview. 'The raw materials for most perfumes came from India,' Lutens said. 'Indian and Arab cultures have a deep-rooted tradition of perfume.'[2] There is a lyrical 2012 book by James McHugh called *Sandalwood and Carrion: Smell in Indian Religion and Culture*,[3] which talks about how ancient Indians didn't discriminate between 'good' and 'bad' smells, and describes all the smells that surrounded our ancestors. Yes, I am a bit obsessed with scents, perfumes and smell.

I am not versed in Hindu philosophy. But one concept I find fascinating is how Hindu and Buddhist faiths linked the term 'vasanas' to thought imprints carried across time. Vasanas means smell in many south Indian languages but alludes to past impressions, even from past lives, that influence present behaviour. It is sometimes called karmic tendencies.

D.T. Suzuki, in his 1930 book, *Studies in The Lankavatara Sutra*, says, 'Vasana literally means "perfuming," or "fumigation,"[4] that is, it is a kind of energy that is left behind when an act is accomplished and has the power to rekindle the old and seek out new impressions.'

So go ahead, pull out that bottle from the back of your cupboard. Douse yourself, if possible, in layers. Enjoy the perfume rather than just spraying some on. And smell stuff. Just go ahead and sniff, like dogs do.

76

Do What AI Cannot: Write Poetry

LET ME ASK YOU this: if you had to pick one trait that was fundamental to the creative process, what would it be? Genius is an obvious one. The problem is that genius is hard to cultivate. Vexingly, you have to be born with it; be an autodidact or, on occasion, as in the case with Van Gogh, certifiably manic-depressive.

The other term that often comes up when talking about creativity is curiosity. Be curious like a child, folks say. Cultivate a Zen mindset, a beginner's mind (always look at things with the curiosity of a beginner).

Curiosity is a choice that is hard to engage in, given the information and sensory overload that assault us every day. How does one cultivate curiosity, when everything that one has to know, needs to know, or doesn't want to know, stares one in the face as it scrolls through Instagram.

Curiosity implies a quest, or at least a voluntary search on Google. However, that may seem redundant as every piece of useful and useless information is handed to you unasked. Children somehow, manage to stay curious, although I would argue that the age is shrinking. No more chasing bubbles; instead it is chasing the iPad.

For adults though, it is all about processing so much readily available information. Let us set developing curiosity aside, shall we? It is an impossible goal to achieve in ten days or less.

I believe that the ability to connect disparate concepts in new and unusual ways is key to creative thinking. In a book published in 2025, titled *The Human Edge: Analogy and the Roots of Creative Intelligence*, cognitive scientist and poet Keith Holyoak examines the essential role analogies play in our capacity for creativity and problem-solving.

In an interview with MIT Press Reader,[1] he describes the difference between AI and the human mind. Sure, AI and large language models (LLMs) can solve novel problems at the college-student level. Today, the reflex for any question is to ask ChatGPT for answers. And you can see why. Princeton University cognitive scientist Tom Griffiths highlights a fundamental human constraint, we humans have a finite capacity in three areas: time, computation and communication.[2] If we have one life and one mind, however complex, how can we share the knowledge with the whole world? AI does it infinitely better because it gathers all available human knowledge.

Creativity, though, is different. As Holyoke says,

> Particularly in the case of artistic creativity, AI faces what may well be an insurmountable limit. In most forms of art—perhaps most obviously music and lyric poetry—the essential point is for the creator to convey an emotional experience to their audience through the medium of their artistic creation. AI has none of this—no emotions, no consciousness, and no individuality. In fact, the general complaint about AI-generated products, whether in the form of writing, music, or visual art, is that they have no soul—no expression of their own emotions or of an individual point of view.

So, write poetry. Think of analogies. They may be our sword against AI and also our salvation.

How do we do this?

The dictionary defines an analogy as the similarity between things that are otherwise dissimilar: a pressure cooker and a bald eagle, for instance. Bet you cannot come up with an analogy connecting the two, although the bald eagles in my neighbourhood are having their blood pressure go up thanks to the encroachment of their habitat. Sounds rather silly, doesn't it? And this, despite my best efforts.

Analogies are hard. I have trouble creating them. Oh, I come up with all the usual ones: flitting like a butterfly, as focused as a hunting tiger, and other clichés. These aren't analogies; they are apologies of analogies. Coming up with a proper analogy involves a three-step process. First, figure out the two things that you want to create an analogy with. For instance, do you want to compare a subway to a submarine? Or are they too similar? How about a subway and blowing your nose?

If you can explain why riding the subway is like blowing your nose, you have a good analogy in the making. You would then list all the qualities of blowing your nose. What does it feel like? What does it look like? You would do the same for riding the subway. With these two lists in hand, all that remains is figuring out how to connect them. The danger is that by the end of this exercise, you will have given up on analogies altogether.

77

Oil Yourself and, If You Like, Your Spouse and Kids as Well

OILS ARE A PHARMACOPEIA for Indians. Sesame oil, especially, is a cure-all. Tamilians coat the insides of their nostrils with sesame oil to lubricate them during Chennai's winter and to prevent colds. When the instructor urges us to think of something relaxing during my meditation class, I think of oils. I visualize a small katori of fragrant honey-coloured sesame oil being emptied on my head just as my grandmother used to do every year on Deepavali.

It wasn't always this way. Oils and I have had a chequered history. While growing up, my grandmother applied coconut oil to my hair and braided it into twin serpents that coiled down my back. Once a week, the whole household had an oil bath—you massaged oil from head to toe; the children had parents or other elderlies help them apply it and wash it off—a ritual that I hated with all my heart.

The prelude went like this: on Sunday mornings, even when I was old enough to sit down to my morning coffee, my grandmother would come up behind me stealthily and apply a handful of warm sesame oil on my head. She had boiled that oil overnight in a copper pot, along with crushed peppercorns and tulsi leaves to remove toxins and purify it. Then, she added dried orange peel so that the oil was suffused with citrusy scents.

I loved the scent but hated the quantity applied to my head. My grandmother didn't believe in the concept of a light hand, and soon beads of oil would roll down my forehead and drip onto the morning paper.

She saved the worst for last. Right after the head massage, she would open my mouth and pop in a large tablespoonful of castor oil just when I finished my fragrant morning coffee. With suddenly strong arms, she would hold my mouth closed till I swallowed the oil. Within minutes, the castor oil, a mild laxative, would take effect, and I would run to the toilet. The entire family got grandmother's castor-oil treatment on Sundays.

Indians also massage oil on babies, and almost uniformly. It seems to me, the babies hate it. I have watched infants howling ferociously as a family matriarch rubs them down. Their slithering arms and legs, as they lie helplessly on a plastic sheet basking in the sun before their bath, make them look like irritated octopuses.

As toddlers, after our oil rubdown, we were wrapped in light towels and shooed into the backyard to soak under the sun for the prescribed half-hour. My father would water his plants, my brother would toss a ball, my mother would yell instructions at the cook, and I would sulk.

Finally, my grandmother would lead me to the bathroom where she would rub on my hair a concoction of ground hibiscus flowers (for hair lustre), shikakai powder (to remove the oil), ground fenugreek seeds (for softness) and lemon peels (to condition). The adults in the family were allowed to wash their own hair, but we kids had to sit ignominiously on a slippery, weathered oil-stool while my grandmother beat the oil out of our hair, much as one beats a drum. Accompanying this was a monologue chiding us for the week's mistakes.

South Indian homes are bathed in oil. Their aromas permeate the house. Oils provide the siren song for some signature dishes like the south Indian aviyal or milagai podi. In Middle Eastern cultures, za'atar and olive oil with warm pita bread provide many an afternoon repast.

Oils provide critical fats to our bodies, and no, that is not an oxymoron. These critical fats, in turn, provide energy, serve as padding or insulation around vital organs, help conserve body heat, transport fat-soluble vitamins through the blood, promote the growth of cells, tissues, and organs, and improve the taste of food. Oils provide essential fatty acids (EFAs) as important as vitamins and minerals. Our bodies cannot synthesize EFAs, so you have to must oils and nuts to get these nutrients.

Go ahead, recreate your childhood. Take those weekly oil-baths. Apply oil on your face and body. If possible, drizzle coconut oil on your breakfast. Why spend on expensive moisturizers when we have the Ayurvedic tradition of abhyanga (oil massage)? And please, don't wait for some Western Instagram influencer to tell you the virtues of oil massage before you decide to follow it.

78

Keep a Journal

OKAY, I FEEL THAT the time has come to clarify that I don't do all the things I prescribe in this book—certainly not every single day. For instance, I don't lunge in the elevator daily as I have suggested. But I have definitely done it, and I'll do it again. Similarly, I have kept a journal, though not with strict regularity, but whenever the mood has taken me.

Many people write a journal for five minutes every morning to take stock of their lives and stay in touch with their feelings. But for others, the idea of keeping a journal seems onerous.

If you are one of those who cannot fathom how to journal, the trick is not to overthink. In fact, if there is one rule I would like to pass on with this book, it would be: don't overthink. Just do.

How to write a journal? Well, you kept a diary as a child, right? In which you wrote about your sibling fights, teenage crushes and feelings? If you didn't and are a journal newbie, here's what you do. Visualize the incident that you want to write about in your head. It may be the tennis match you played today or the fall you took. What is the first and most striking image that comes to mind? Write about it.

Try to approach it differently. If you are writing about your violin class, write about the feel of the violin rather than the clichéd sounds you heard in the studio. If you are writing about a basketball court, write about how the court smells rather than following the usual description of what you see.

Describe events in which you failed and how you overcame them. Rather than describing your failure in generic terms such as 'obstacles' and 'overcoming challenges', make it personal and specific. Write poetry. Nobody is going to read it anyway.

You are telling a story: *your* story. Use the storytelling techniques of balance, conflict and resolution to make a point in a particular paragraph or for the whole story.

We live to tell stories. We make sense of life by telling them. We connect to people through stories. Why not write your in a journal?

79

What's Your Poison?

THIS IS A BOOK on health, so I am not referring to cocktails, even though I love them. What do you reach for during the day? Juice, a diet coke, coconut water, a mocktail or wait, what about that drink of yore: the sherbet? It is cooling, light and quintessentially Indian. Sadly, it also seems out of fashion. Prove me wrong.

Are sherbets being overtaken by mocktails? Most restaurants serve mocktails, but few include sherbets in their menu. At home, we all connect sherbets with summer. Drinks infused with hibiscus and rose flowers, sabja seeds and lime.

Before mocktails, we all drank sherbets made of kokum (*Garcinia indica*), mango, screw pine or kewra, khus or vetiver and sugarcane. Mixing a number of ingredients does not a sherbet make. Milk is a no-no in the sherbet category, but it forms the basis of the thandai we all drink.

There are two schools of thought when it comes to summer drinks. The West reaches for instant quick fixes: ice creams, slushes, 'soda' or fizzy drinks and chilled juices. The East is more convoluted. We drink keri ka panna and bael sherbet with a history that goes back to when the Mughals came to India. Some sherbets can trace their lineage and names back to Arabia and Turkey. They all heat or cool the body, depending on the season. For instance, sandalwood is cooling and sandalwood sherbet infused with rose or mogra petals is another visually arresting cooling drink.

I have made a shortcut sherbet that I plan to drink for two months. I submerge a stick of sandalwood in water and float some mogra and rose petals on top. For good measure, I have prepared this concoction in a copper vessel. In two months, I expect that the fountain of youth will have found me. Either that or my hair will turn yellow from all the sandalwood I am imbibing.

Most of our sherbets are made with four ingredients: fruits, flowers, spices and herbs like mint. These are drinks that transport us to our childhood when we came home to chilled seasonal juices and sherbets—red rhododendron in Himachal Pradesh; a delicate green aam panna in Rajasthan; spiced buttermilk in Gujarat and Kerala; red jil jil jigarthanda in Madurai, made of rose syrup and sarsaparilla; Rooh Afza and Rasna coolers all over India; chocolate-coloured panagam in the midst of south Indian weddings; kesar faloodas at Crawford Market in Mumbai, along with the ubiquitous tender coconut water; bael panna in Lucknow; the prized Bengali kaancha-mitha aam ka panna; and a variety of red watermelon-based sherbets in Delhi's Chandni Chowk.

These are the drinks of many an Indian childhood, along with sucking on chuskis and ripe tamarind fruits that grow so profusely on the roadside in south India. Climb up a mango tree, lean back on its branches, allow the wind to rustle your hair and suck on a ripe mango or tamarind fruit. Better yet, drink an imli (tamarind) sherbet, a Bhojpuri barley sattu, a ragi kanji or fresh lime soda. Lace it with vodka, if you must, but switch to juices and sherbets.

80

Engage in Forest Bathing (Even in a City!)

OF ALL THE THINGS that centre and calm you down, being amidst nature has to be close to the top. Being in the sunshine, surrounded by swaying trees, listening to bird calls, and enjoying the warmth of the earth under your bare feet is soothing and refreshing.

For us urban dwellers, the challenge is to find little pockets of nature to enjoy and gain nourishment from. It is possible. Some of us go on long walks through the parks that dot our cities. Others go away to the wildlife preserves on weekends. It doesn't matter. Any activity that allows us to engage with nature fairly consistently is good.

When talking about nature, wildlife or the ecosystem, humans often use the paternalistic and patronizing word, 'fragile', to describe it. We see ourselves as custodians of this planet but are also its most deadly criminals. We conserve and exterminate. We use more resources than any other species and are the planet's apex predator.

This human-centric view is both understandable and wrong. The planet isn't fragile. Life on earth existed long before humans got here, and will likely continue. The engine of evolution will continue in spite of human intervention. This so-called fragile planet, in other words, isn't waiting with bated breath for humans to save it. It couldn't care less.

Humans need wildlife, not because of some misconstrued sense of noblesse oblige, but because nature is central to our existence. We need them more than they need us. The birds, bees, beasts and marine life that surround us, weave a web that is far more complex than we can fathom. This web is far more necessary to our well-being than we have the knowledge or sense to admit. At the very least, nature and wildlife differentiate us as a species.

The connection between humans and forests is ancient and primal. Forests are where we came from, and returning to these wildlife sanctuaries calms us down and makes us feel alive and connected to our planet and ecosystem. Nature heals in mysterious ways. It gives us solace without saying a word. As Anne Frank said, 'The best remedy for those who are afraid, lonely or unhappy is to go outside; somewhere where they can be quite alone with the heavens, nature and God.'[1]

Wild animals show us a way of being that is primitive, yet noble. Their way of life is both alien and yet rises above human constructs such as greed and materialism. We in India are lucky to have not just the world's largest population of tigers but also the only surviving population of the Asiatic lion in Gir forest. We have snow leopards in Hemis National Park, barasingha deer in Kanha and two-thirds of the world's one-horned rhinos in Kaziranga. We need them to show us another approach to living.

Our natural habitat holds the greatest expression of life on earth. As ethnobotanist Mark Plotkin said in his TED talk,[2] our forests hold answers to questions that we have yet to ask. Till we figure out the questions, we need to hold on to our forests.

So, get out. Go to the nearest wildlife park or nature reserve. The fresh air will clear cobwebs from your soul and do you good.

81

Sat-Chit-Ananda: Follow Your Bliss but Find It First

MY MIND HAS RECENTLY been full of sobering thoughts about death, taxes, ageing and the question of how to age gracefully.

The literature on ageing lists many activities that can help us as we get older. Exercise is an obvious one, as is developing a close and nurturing group of friends and family. There is one virtue, however, that is underplayed in many studies about ageing and that is cultivating a passion. This isn't easy to do, mostly because we don't realize its importance until we are too old.

Most adults attempt to live rich and fulfilling lives. Look around at your friends and colleagues. They all probably have jobs that are sometimes tedious but mostly engaging. They have hobbies, such as playing golf or tennis, reading a bit before sleeping and following a few television shows. They have social networks, they go to restaurants and maintain friendships. As do you.

What many of us lack, though is a passion that we can turn to. Work doesn't count unless it can be parlayed after retirement. If you are an art historian, for instance, you can still be engaged in art studies after retirement.

I know a few people who have this passion for a particular activity. My late brother-in-law in Florida was a physician with a busy private practice. His weekends, however, were devoted to his passion: epigraphy or the study of ancient inscriptions. He collected data on the Indus Valley civilization and its scripts. He read reams of literature, talked to scholars from all over the world via Skype, attended conferences and took online courses. Sometimes, an entire weekend would go by without him ever leaving his library.

But what about the rest of us? Perhaps the way to find a solution is to imbue the question with some urgency.

Think about it this way: who will hang out with you when you are eighty? No matter how affectionate our children are, there comes a point when they are too busy for us, and often, this point comes sooner than we want.

Ageing involves solitude whether you like it or not. Your world shrinks, your friends die, and you have to figure out how to keep your mind occupied. Cheery thought, isn't it?

Sailing through the choppy waters of advanced age involves figuring out an activity to engage and energize you. Music, for instance, offers great potential for relaxation. The way to convert this into a passion is to take music appreciation courses.

Similarly, playing chess does not require you to do heavy lifting. It can be played with any child that walks through the door.

If you happen to be spiritually inclined, this is the time to take a deep dive into your religion because at the end of the day, we all have to confront questions about our maker and our role in this world.

Ageing gracefully does not only mean slathering on expensive creams and lotions. If you find a passion, it can just as easily involve mental somersaults that will leave you refreshed and glad to be alive.

Oh, and also, learn the pleasures of silence and solitude because, like it or not, all of us are going to experience lots of it as we age.

82

Use the Alexander Technique

THERE IS A GREAT scene in the movie *The Other Guys* (2010) where actor Mark Wahlberg pumps his arms up and down and shouts, 'I want to be a peacock!' His chicken-like pose works for the movie but is totally wrong in the real world. Peacocks don't flail their wings and jump up and down like Wahlberg did. They are more like haughty divas on the catwalk than irate cops jumping up and down.

Have you ever wondered about good posture in animals? About how a giraffe maintains its poise in spite of such an ungainly long neck? About how a porcupine, which looks horrendously ill-proportioned (big body, tiny legs) but manages to run elegantly?

Harvard University professor emeritus Dr Andrew Biewener studied animal locomotion: how grebes run over water; how pigeons negotiate obstacles; and how wallabies hop. One of Dr Biewener's early discoveries was on how large animals with relatively small bones and muscles could move so elegantly, without overloading their skeletons. The reason: good posture.

Have you seen a peacock in the wild? Have you seen how long and stretched its neck seems to be? Ballet teachers often tell their students to stand tall, as though a rope was tugging upwards at their head, thus elongating their spine. Peacocks stand this way.

The Alexander Technique, developed by Australian actor and singer Frederick Mathias Alexander in 1910, still continues to be in robust use today across the world.[1] What began as a way to teach actors to project their voices, also operates on the principle of an elongated spine. So how do you elongate your spine and stand tall? By reminding yourself to do so throughout the day is a good start! While it is best to learn this from a professional Alexander Technique (henceforth to be called AT) practitioner, here is a sense of what it will do to you.

Are you, dear reader, staring at these words on screen or on paper? Now, just for a minute, pause and pay attention to your body. Where are you holding the tension? I realize that I unconsciously clench my jaw, tighten my scalp and tense my eyes—which, it turns out, is something we all do when staring at computer screens. Over days, weeks and years, these muscle memories add up.

The lithe lady beside me is trying to undo a lifetime of bad muscular habits. Her name is Padmini Menon, and she has the softest touch I have experienced. Her voice, too, is sing-song, like a lullaby, as we stand in her small study in Indiranagar, Bengaluru. Menon has her hands on the back of my head and is attempting, just through her touch, to do two seemingly contradictory things: to release and lengthen my body.

Over the course of half an hour, Menon's hand touches my neck a lot. She coaxes my back and neck into 'releasing,' as she describes it. She asks me to lie on my back on a flat, hard bed in a 'semi-supine' position. This, I learnt, is a great way to retrain the body and one that is beloved by AT practitioners.

It is called a 'position of mechanical advantage.' What you do is lie flat, place a couple of books under your head, bend your legs so your knees point at the ceiling and place your folded hands on your belly. And then you consciously, if quietly, tell your body to release itself and work with gravity.

Menon, who has been practising AT since 2008, makes me lie down, sit on a chair and then stand. That is pretty much all we do during the course of the three sessions. But God, as architect Ludwig Mies van der Rohe said, is in the details. How you sit, how you stand, how you walk, it all matters. At one point, Menon holds my hand in hers and stands motionless. What are you doing, I ask.

'I am easing my body so that it will influence your body to ease yours,' she replies. 'Your body listens to my words, but intuitively, it responds to my touch,' she says.

This is how a session goes. Essentially, the goal is to soften and lengthen your body. To be at ease, to use the optimal amount of energy needed for a task.

83

Frame Your World with the Right Words

MOST POLITICIANS AND LEADERS are adept at what psychology calls 'framing'. Framing is how you see the world and make your decisions. Stimuli come at you from all sides. On your way up the corporate or political ladder, people tell you things; they call you names to your face. How you process this input—or rather how you 'frame' this input—is up to you.

We all frame the world all the time. It is a 'cognitive bias' that was first brought to light by economists Daniel Kahneman and Amos Tversky in their 1974 paper, 'Judgment Under Uncertainty: Heuristics and Biases'.[1] When we say that we are putting our dog 'to sleep' instead of killing it, that is framing—a way of coming to terms with something awful. When we say the boyfriend broke up with us, rather than 'he dumped me', that, too, is framing reality to suit our mental frame.

Salespeople take advantage of our desire to frame reality by putting three shirts beside each other—one for ₹2,000, another for ₹5,000, and the third for ₹10,000. Suddenly, the middle one seems reasonable, and you walk out with it, though you don't need it.

Memory researcher Elizabeth Loftus has proved that simply replacing a word can alter a reaction. In 1974, she conducted the 'Car Crash Experiment', later cited by numerous memory researchers.[2] When witnesses to a car accident were asked, 'How fast was the car going when it smashed into the victims?' they would give higher speeds than if the question simply said, 'How fast was the car going when it hit the victims?' That's framing. Put another way, there is no 'one' reality. It all depends on how you see the world.

For example, let us consider how the late politician J. Jayalalithaa, erstwhile chief minister of Tamil Nadu, used framing. The reason Jayalalithaa was so good, and lasted long in the pugnacious, sometimes puerile world of Tamil Nadu politics, was because she learnt to frame the world to suit her ideology, to convert insults into infomercials.

She learnt this not as chief minister but on the way up when she was a stumbling starlet and novice politician. She learnt it early on when men in starched dhotis called her names. She learnt it when men in her own party treated her with contempt and eventually betrayed her, and when the public ousted her even though she believed she was doing her best to help them, and even when the courts had her arrested.

Along the way, she cultivated a thick skin and political savvy. She made enemies and gained resilience. She took control and got even. She settled scores without flinching. She wore body armour when the death threats came fast and furious. Quite simply, Jayalalithaa learnt to convert her rage into rhetoric. And what rhetoric it was. She wasn't in the same league as Prime Minister Modi, who speaks without a script. But Jayalalithaa knew how to use metaphor and timing. She spoke with gravitas and used powerful examples to frame her message.

'Only the mother knows what her children need,' she said at an election rally in Virudhachalam, riffing on her title 'Amma', which means mother.

To convert politics into benevolent motherhood is the power of framing.

84

Keep Your Mouth Shut

SILENCE IS AN UNDERRATED tool in the arsenal of parenting. So far, I have only used it to give the silent treatment to erring preteens. This time, I plan to use a different approach. It involves pausing before every uttered instruction, quickly figuring out if I really need to utter that instruction, and hopefully not saying anything at all.

As a mother, I plan to do what every married man learns to do pretty early on in the marriage: listen, nod and remain silent.

Silence is also the latest practice to hit the spectrum of thought exercises that began with meditation and mindfulness and then moved on to gratitude, loving-kindness meditation, cognitive behavioural therapy and self-compassion. The goal of all these exercises is to soften and shape the mind as if it were a clay sculpture.

Silence is both a latecomer to this party, as well as being one of the oldest. From Vedic rishis to Benedictine monks, from Sufi saints to Buddhist teachers, every faith has used silence to access spirituality, compassion and centring of the mind.

And yet, silence—like mothers, I might add—has been underappreciated in the modern arsenal of mind-body practices, until now.

Amazon is building a giant nature preserve to encourage its employees to take time off to walk in silence. It hopes these silent walks will encourage creative thinking among its employees, who they hope will come up with world-changing ideas.

Companies are scrambling for ways to empower and encourage employees not just to be more productive but also to think brilliantly and not burn out. Perhaps an hour of silence in the office may help.

My own experiment with silence hasn't begun well, mostly because I have set myself an impossible goal. I will be silent while my daughter drives our car. She enrolled in a driving school for a month rather than enduring parental questions, doubts and instructions.

To execute my new resolution and her novice driving skills, we set off early in the morning for a drive to St Mark's Road. She turned into the road, I clenched my fist and my mind screamed: 'She is too close to the car on the left, she isn't anticipating the darting stray dogs and scooters, she is driving too fast, braking too hard, not driving fast enough …'

But, I was proud of myself, for I uttered nothing. None of the above made their way out of my mouth. There was silence in the car. At the end of our drive, my daughter got out and smiled through stiff lips. At least this time, I hadn't made her cry.

The first time we drove together (before she enrolled in a driving school), I kept lifting the emergency brake and kept up a litany of screaming instructions. 'Look out. You are too close to the car in front. Slow down. SLOW DOWN. Press the brake.'

'Ma, stop it. You are making me nervous,' she cried, literally, with tears threatening to spill out.

After a few iterations, I decided on the silence protocol. It was among the hardest things I have done. Essentially, it involves biting your tongue, so you don't speak. Sure, my blood pressure went up. Sure, I clenched my fist till I drew blood. But at least I wasn't reprimanding my child. And she drove better.

85

Don't Use Maps

THE MOST EXCITING DEVELOPMENTS in brain research—itself an exciting field—today have to do with neuroplasticity and neurogenesis. Think of our brain as a giant plastic ball. Researchers want to pull and push it, mould it into suppleness, make it nimble and bounce it back into youthful health.

A 2023 survey paper by researchers in Pakistan, India, Nepal and Italy, titled 'Innovative Approaches and Therapies to Enhance Neuroplasticity and Promote Recovery in Patients With Neurological Disorders: A Narrative Review,'[1] talks about the many approaches including Virtual and Augmented Reality tools, robotics, biofeedback, pharmacology, exercise, sleep and cognitive enhancement techniques.

Neuroplasticity alludes to brain adaptability. Neurogenesis, or the growth of new neurons, happens as a matter of course during prenatal development. Neurons continue to proliferate like crazy while we learn to crawl, stand, walk and run. This regeneration slows down considerably as we age.

Adult neurogenesis was considered to be non-existent till the mid-1980s. Today, it is established that exercise, proper sleep and, yes, certain drugs (cannabinoids) can help neural stem cells generate. The exact ways in which the size and growth of the hippocampus can be stimulated are still being explored.

There is broad consensus among experts that physical exercise offers a wide spectrum of benefits, including increasing the size of the hippocampus, the section of the brain associated with emotion, memory and the autonomic nervous system. Some studies show that picking up a demanding hobby, like playing tennis or the violin, can cause the brain to regenerate.

The trick is to incorporate these new findings in brain research into our lives.

Heard of geo-caching? An article in *Harvard Health*, talks about how going into uncharted territory without a map forces the brain to work in multiple ways.[2] We have to learn how to orient ourselves geo-spatially, learn to spot landmarks, remember the routes so we can come back and much more.

Next time you need to go to a new place within your city, don't turn on your trusted 'Maps' app that tells you every direction. Instead, do it the old-fashioned way. Look up the directions before you leave home and try to go. Then try to come back.

This is called 'Orienteering' and there are groups for this in the US. 'Orienteering is the sport of navigation—often held in unfamiliar terrain—using a map and compass. It's easy to learn and a fun way to exercise your body and mind as you enjoy the outdoors.'[3]

Sounds good, doesn't it?

86

Surrender to the Muse

IN A TED TALK, author Elizabeth Gilbert explained how the ancients didn't view a person as a genius.[1] Rather, genius was an insight that came to people when they were in a heightened state of awareness; when they were relaxed enough to listen to the messages that the universe was sending them; when their minds were free and their consciousness expanded enough to connect disparate ideas. It is this that is the core of all creativity, offers grist for ideas and turns people into geniuses.

The question facing us average, non-genius human beings, is how to enhance this awareness and become attuned to new ideas. How can we be of open mind and relaxed spirit so that the inner voice, that whispers its secrets to us, can be heard?

The rules for Sanskrit poetry, for instance, list three qualities necessary for a good poet: pratibha (poetic genius), vyutpatti (knowledge or learning) and abhyasa (effort).

Effort and learning can be cultivated through training. But poetic genius—that elusive flash of insight that raises a work from the realms of great to extraordinary—comes from a fickle muse and is not easy to achieve consistently. History reveals that people used many different ways. Ancient Romans used to watch the flight of birds to figure out patterns that portended the future. They called this augury. The most famous example is Rome's founding story, in which the twins Romulus and Remus each wanted to build the city of Rome in two different spots: Romulus on Palatine Hill and Remus on Aventine Hill. They set up 'augural tents' in different spots and watched the sky. Remus saw six vultures, but Romulus saw twelve and went on to build the city that even today bears his name.

Divining, using birds and animals, remained part of most ancient civilizations. Now, as I stand on my balcony every day and watch birds, I see wagtails, bulbuls, sunbirds and black kites. They flit about the trees and glide in the sky. But I don't have the patience or stillness to observe patterns in their movements and glean omens from these patterns. That requires the still expansiveness that monks cultivate. That requires silencing the mind's chatter so that clarity can percolate through. Today, instead of omens, we use apps to guide whether to embark on a particular project.

This is the problem with stillness and surrender in an age of noise. Most of us don't know how to experience, process, use or embrace stillness. Until I embarked on this project, I didn't think of surrender as a way to creativity and clarity.

My default mode during any lull in the day was to whip out my phone and recheck the message that I had sent one minute ago, waiting for the addictive jolt of a reply. The immediate gratification from every Instagram or Facebook 'like' and the replies on X, leaves little room for the long haul that is the road to quieting the mind. I am still a novice at this. Every day (well, not every day), I sit on a mat, attempt stillness and surrender and think: now what?

In his influential book, *Silence: The Power of Quiet in a World Full of Noise*, Thich Nhat Hanh, describes five kinds of sounds that arise from silence. The first, he says, is the 'wonderful sound', the sound of the 'wonders of life that are calling you'. The second is the 'Sound of the one who observes the world'. The third is the Brahma sound—the sound of creation. The fourth is the 'sound of the rising tide', or the voice of the Buddha. The fifth is the 'sound that transcends all sounds of the world'.[2]

I sat for half an hour waiting to hear these sounds and only heard a car reversing, a muezzin calling, a parakeet screeching, my neighbour yelling at her maid and a horn tooting. I have miles to go and promises to keep before I can hear the sounds of the silences that Hanh is talking about. So, I do the next best thing: I throw money at the problem.

My noise-cancelling headphones are amazing. They allow me to stay in silence in the middle of the constant noise that is the melody of

India. I put them on one afternoon while stuck in a traffic jam. Having spent money on them, I ought to make them count, and if not, begin to listen to inner silence, to at least think deeply.

I want to declutter my head and allow my innermost desires to rise. Caught in the maelstrom of life, I have suppressed reflection for so long that I no longer know how to go about it. The only thing to do is surrender to the muse and wait for ideas to percolate.

So can you if you incorporate stillness into your life. Perhaps on a long car ride to the other side of the city or while sitting in the Metro. Just be still, won't you?

87

Pen Down Your Dreams

IN A 2008 PROFILE that I wrote for the *Mint* newspaper, Nandan Nilekani once told me about his process of reflection.[1] Every few months, he said, he sat with a piece of paper pretty much by himself and reflected on the past and what goals he wanted to achieve in the future.

'How will you know if your dream has come true if you don't even know what your dreams are?' asked a friend.

Dreams are easy to figure out. Amorphous and ethereal, they don't need any connection with reality. I dream of doing somersaults. I dream of being in the circus—specifically, a trapeze artist. I dream of owning an Hermès Jypsiere bag in orange. I dream of spending a month in Burgundy drinking DRC wines, then moving to Bordeaux and drinking all the big five: Latour, Margaux, Lafite, Mouton Rothschild and Haut Brion. I dream of dancing the tango in Argentina, preferably with Antonio Banderas, and driving down the German Autobahn in a Tesla convertible.

Dreams are easy. It is the goals that I have trouble with. Goals need to be accountable, measurable, and have some link with reality. So, I sat in silence one day, a blank sheet in my hands, and confronted my fears. I realized that the trouble with vocalizing what I want was that I would have to work hard.

You may want to speak fluent French, but will you put in the effort it takes to learn it?

A small step towards your goal is to write it down.

88

Marry Your Cellphone

'I AM THINKING OF marrying my cell phone,' I tell my husband. We are sitting beside each other, tapping on our colour-coded iPads—his, black, and mine Hermès orange—the colour, not the brand. 'Oh really,' he says in that overly enthusiastic voice he affects when he hasn't heard a word I have said.

My inspiration is Aaron Chervenak, a Los Angeles man who, in 2016, drove to Las Vegas and married his smartphone, complete with a ring and a priest who proclaimed them 'husband and cell phone'. Documented and uploaded on YouTube, the marriage isn't legal. But that, according to Chervenak, is a small price to pay to declare his undying love for what is, for many of us, our favourite appendage.[1]

'If we're gonna be honest with ourselves, we connect with our phones on so many emotional levels,' says Chervenak in the YouTube video. 'We look to it for solace, to calm us down, to put us to sleep, to ease our minds; to me, that's also what a relationship is about. So, in a sense, my smartphone has been my longest relationship. That's why I decided to see what it was like to actually marry a phone.'

The man is right. Our relationship with our devices is complicated. More addictive than marijuana, more trance-inducing than a politician's trump speech, our gadgets punctuate our lives and burrow deep into our souls. In a sense, they define us. Look at Chernevak's list. There is an app for every emotion. For solace, there is MoodKit. For calm, you can meditate through the app Calm or Headspace. To sleep, there are lulling nature sounds, music or podcasts. To ease your mind, there are a million games. There are countless others. I use Grid Diary for journalling, the 7 Minutes Workout to exercise, BrainHQ to focus, Freedom and SelfControl to stop distractions, and 50 Languages to learn Kannada. On average, I touch my device more often than my spouse.

'I think I will elope and marry my smartphone,' I say loudly.

This time, he looks up with that deer-caught-in-the-headlights look that I have come to recognize. I can hear the wheels whirring in his head as he processes this bizarre statement sans preamble or context. I know what he is thinking: What have I done, and what is the best response?

I even know what he will say, for it would have been my approach. When you don't know how you have messed up, offence is the best form of defence. 'Well, you certainly pay more attention to your phone than you do to me,' he says huffily.

'At least the phone is a smart one,' I retort, and I mean it to sting.

And so, it comes to this. You have been married for so long that you can hear each other think, and the object of your jealousy, the mistress in your ménage à trois, is a device that rings instead of purring, that buzzes in lieu of flirting.

Viewed through this prism, marrying your cell phone is the logical next step and a little sad. Will Chervenak's bride put up with it when he upgrades to the next model? Will he leave her for someone from a different species?

On 3 December 1992, the first text message was sent over a phone—'Merry Christmas.' The late Finnish engineer Matti Makkonen pitched the idea of a 'short messaging service' at a telecoms conference in Copenhagen. Nokia incorporated the idea into its phones; the rest is history—at least over a trillion messages sent per year.

Remember voicemail—that quaint, outdated thing we used to do? I love voicemails and try to leave some to friends and family through WhatsApp or iPhones. But they don't appreciate my cutesy messages because they are an intrusion. Reading a text can be done surreptitiously while bored in a boardroom. Listening to voicemail requires headphones and solitude.

In the new reality, communication is condensed for efficiency and speed. Letters replace words (R u ok?); emoticons replace the emotions that leak through your voice when you actually speak to people or leave voicemail. Texting, unlike live conversation, offers a great buffer. If someone asks you an uncomfortable question, you don't have to respond. The surprise or pain you feel will not be apparent to the other person. You can fake a response by sending a 'thumbs up' emoji when you actually want to kill yourself and the other person.

Nowhere is this more apparent than in today's teenagers. They know how to pose thanks to selfies: pouty fish lips for girls and macho glares behind glares (sunglasses) for the boys. They are camera-savvy, intuitively understanding composition and light. Facebook is waning in popularity among preteens. They prefer the casualness of Snapchat and the texture of Instagram. A thousand words typed on Facebook Messenger cannot convey the mood of a party as effectively as an Instagram photo.

There are many instances when communicating via a device is an excellent option. When you have to spring things on unsuspecting spouses, there is no better friend than a cell phone. Consider this message: '5 friends showing up at home. Know you have world cup finals. Thought u r going to friend's house to watch so agreed. Hope ok.' Can you imagine springing this on your spouse in person? Through texts, you can escape his curses.

Or consider this message to your son or daughter. 'Why are you not picking up the phone? You will be grounded if you do not answer my call. I am serious. And by the way, you have to attend the wedding of that cousin you hate next week with us.' Offence before defence always, my friends, particularly with children. Yell at them before forcing them to do stuff they detest.

And now I need to reconnect with my to-be spouse. There are messages to read, emojis to craft, photos to share, and miles to go before I sleep.

89

Be a Gardener Instead of a Carpenter

IN *THE GARDENER AND the Carpenter*, Alison Gopnik wisely points out, what the new science of child development tells us about the relationship between parents and children, and the two ways to parent.[1] The carpenter believes that he can sculpt his child through instruction, criticism and specific activities or goals into something that he envisions them to be. The gardener simply lays the framework in which plants—in this case, children—can thrive.

We all intuitively want to be gardeners, gently tending our flock of children so that they become the best they can be. In this scenario, we lay the groundwork for them to grow.

The reality of daily parenting, however, is more carpenter than a gardener, more screaming coach than a compassionate nurturer. It is a litany of instructions rather than setting the scene for growth. Taking a deep breath and holding your tongue can help balance this out.

This is difficult because we have to subdue the eighteen muscles required for articulation, including the pharyngeal, glottal, epiglottal, apical and radical. The tongue is the most important organ in speech. To tie it up requires an act of will.

For me, what helped restrain my tongue was humming. Yes, really. After all, the earliest type of speech was called musillanguage.[2] According to one stream of thinking, language evolved from the guttural sounds humans made when they experienced emotions. From our early sounds of weeping and shouts of happiness came the variation of tones that evolved parallelly into music and language. That's the hypothesis, anyway.

So, I decided to hum every time I felt like advising, instructing or suggesting things to my children and indeed, my spouse. This stance was the last refuge of my tortured mind and went against everything that I wanted to do. After all, the human instinct is to encode thoughts into words. Of what use these words if you cannot speak them?

Things are getting better, though. I am learning to pause before I speak. I am learning to hold back the conversion of thought into spoken word. I am learning to embrace and, indeed, revel in being mute.

I wish I could tell you that it has made me wiser or solved all the mother–daughter quarrels in our household. But what it has done is give both sides some respite.

When I don't snap to judgement or swiftly bark orders, it gives my kids the space to choose, decide and safely make mistakes. I have discovered that they are surprisingly good at making choices. They weigh and judge consequences, act swiftly when needed and, most delightful of all, aren't always in danger of self-destructing.

This, then, is the mother's delusion, isn't it? That things will fall apart if we aren't around, things are always better when we do it and our kids need us at every step of their lives.

Proactive parenting is the philosophy I have espoused for most of my life. To my shock, pulling back has been the best thing for my kids.

90
Hug Trees

SANSKRIT POETRY DESCRIBES A sublime connection between humans and nature. There is a delightful tradition called 'dohada', which views trees as pregnant before flowering. Kalidasa's *Ritusamhara* and epics like the Mahabharata and the Ramayana, all touch upon this link between humans—specifically women—and trees.

As described by Maurice Bloomfield in a 1920 article, 'The Dohada or Craving of Pregnant Women: A Motif of Hindu Fiction',[1] Hindu prosody has come up with an 'exquisite notion of this sudden blossoming of trees in the springtime preceded by a pregnancy fancy'.

Different trees have different whims. The Ashoka tree likes to be kicked by dancing girls as a prod for it to flower. The champaka tree bursts into a bud when sprinkled with perfumed water. And, my favourite, the bakula tree blooms when it is sprinkled with wine from the liquor-addled lips of gazelle-eyed maidens.

After reading this, I tried spitting a California Chardonnay on the bark of a creeping Madurai jasmine on my terrace, but it didn't burst into bloom. Must have been the bad wine.

But I, like many Bengalureans, do hug and kick trees whenever I can—like the Salabhanjika woman portrayed in sculptures. You know, the kind seen all over India, in temples and archaeological sites? 'Moon-breasted, swan-waisted and elephant-hipped,' as poetry would have it. These women stand in the seductive tribhanga or three-angled pose, often leaning against a creeping saal tree, hence the name, Salabhanjika: 'she who breaks off the bough of a saal tree to make the tree bloom'.

It isn't just women, though, who are modern-day Salabhanjikas. Prem Koshy, owner of the iconic Bengaluru café—Koshy's—once climbed atop a mahogany tree opposite his café to protect it from municipal workers who wanted to cut down the tree and widen the road. Koshy refused to come down. The tree still stands, and he distributes mahogany seeds to interested customers.

'Trees are angels of silence,' says Krishna, noted birder and ecologist, when we finally catch up with him. Watch a raintree close its leaves and become still at dusk; you will understand what he means.

I know gardeners who sing to their plants, even though Daniel Chamovitz, in his 2012 book, *What a Plant Knows*, writes that plants are deaf and cannot hear Bach—or Beyoncé. Plants live in silence. They feel but don't hear. They communicate through pheromones and chemicals. Humans do, too, when you think about it—particularly when falling in love. This is why we share good chemistry with some folks—and hopefully, it includes our spouses—and not with others. Chemistry doesn't need words. Experts in non-verbal communication suggest that gestures and eye contact communicate far more than speech. Words, as the cliché goes, are cheap.

So, every now and then, find a broad banyan or acacia tree. Hug it. Try to hear what this tree is saying. It has probably eaves-dropped on conversations, marriage proposals and political scams. What does it know? What is it saying?

91

Roar like a Lion

ANIMALS ARE EXTRAORDINARILY EFFICIENT at communication. They use their voices for a purpose. A lion roars to claim territory or victory. Deer give alarm calls to warn their neighbours about nearby predators. Coyotes howl at the moon to call their pack back into the fold after a period of individual hunting. Birds sing to impress mates.

In each case, the usage of the voice has a reason. Humans are the only species who use their vocal cords for gossip and diatribe. We speak for many reasons and sometimes for no reason at all. Like my nephew said when I asked him what he and his friends talk about. 'Oh, we spend half an hour discussing Drake (a rapper). Mostly, we talk about nothing at all: games, scores, apps, music, stuff like that.'

Can I channel the efficiency of animals and birds in my speech? Can I use my vocal cords efficiently? Can I roar like a lion?

There is a Sanskrit word, 'sadharanikaran', which is used to describe communication in ancient India. Derived from the Natyashastra, sadharanikaran means 'simplification without dilution', which, you could say, could be the goal of all communication. An interesting 2015 paper by Dr Nandita Kapadia-Kundu, titled '*Sadharanikaran*, A Theory for Social and Health Behavior Change',[1] outlines how early Indians viewed communication. There was context or sandharba; there was communication in specific ways. This model placed 'sahridaya' (compassion filled with affection) at the centre of all communication.

In other words, in order to persuade, you have to induce sahridaya in the other person. Animals do this through their non-verbal communication. We ought to consider it, too.

92

Talk to Elders

WHAT IS YOUR STRATEGY when you meet elders, such as those uncles you encounter at weddings. You sit with them, chat desultorily about their prostate, how hot Mumbai has become and maybe reminisce about the ancestral home or village. The conversation ends abruptly after five minutes, and then both parties, with relief, turn to their devices.

I am taking a different approach, perhaps because I am surrounded by octogenarians. I find that every elder has a secret switch, something that they love, something that is worth sharing, and I will enjoy learning. The trick is to quickly find out what. It could be particle physics, pranic healing, poetry or the parachute regiment. How do you draw them out, if only to make the conversation interesting?

Their career is a good starting point. Questions in this area can be broken down into four ways.

Comparison: 'Uncle, how is the Indian Army different today from when you commanded it?'

Prescription: 'Auntie, if you could influence today's attitude towards weavers and textiles, what would you do?'

Takeaways: 'Uncle, what was your biggest takeaway from your career with RAW (Research and Analysis Wing, India's primary intelligence agency)?'

Rewriting history: 'If you could do something different, what would it be?'

Such questions are uncomfortable to ask and even more uncomfortable for them to confront. These are modest folk. They are not forthcoming and dislike talking about themselves. Often, you meet them in social settings—at parties or weddings—where pleasantries, even if boring, are the norm. They are not used to laser-like questions. As Roger Angell says in his essay, 'This Old Man' in *The New Yorker*, '… we elders have learned a thing or two, including invisibility'.[1] Elders are used to being ignored and talked over. They expect politeness; genuine interest is new for them. In these circumstances, how do you cut to the chase?

It helps if you warm up to the topic. Start by saying that you have been reading about foreign intelligence, textiles, architecture, the behaviour of wasps, or whatever it is that uncle or auntie is an expert at. You have to give them four sentences, at least as a preamble, before springing the question. You have to be prepared for uncomfortable laughter and non-answers. 'Actually, there was no one takeaway, as you call it. We were so busy filling the need of the hour that … well …', the voice trails away.

Women of that generation are trickier, particularly if they have been homemakers. They may ramble and go around in circles. They haven't been exposed to management-speak and bullet points. Their wisdom is homespun, passed along through long anecdotes. They take time to get to the nub of things. You have to slow down and listen.

The question for many is, 'Why bother?'

Why bother hanging around old people? Sometimes, it isn't a choice when your parents live with you, near you, or come to visit. They are around, and you have to talk about something. Sometimes, it is a way of engaging with your relatives or friends' parents. I could tell you that elders give you perspective, but that takes time. So, really, it boils down to not getting bored and figuring out a way to engage your mind by engaging theirs.

Some months ago, at a memorial service for Anne Warrior, the educator who co-founded the Mallya Aditi School in Bengaluru, several people, including her grandson, spoke about Warrior's love of poetry. My grandmother could make anyone love poetry, said her grandson, and I quote from memory.

I used to meet her about once a month when both of us were members of *The Bangalore Black Tie*. We chitchatted. Not once did we speak about poetry. Indeed, I didn't know about her interest in this topic till her memorial service.

How do you pass along a passion? Often, it is simply through presence, conversation and passing remarks. If some subject can give you pleasure in your eighties, would you study it—even if it is 'useless' like classical music, dance or poetry? Is something worth learning, not for an immediate goal but for a gradual moulding of the mind?

Poetry is one of the last bastions of the cultured mind. Schoolchildren memorize poems and then drop poetry once they hit college. I haven't read poetry for decades. I didn't know how to until very recently when I experienced it through the eyes of Warrior and my father. He has unintentionally unpackaged this world in a way that I can access it. When I tell him about a forthcoming trip to Varanasi, he says Ralph Waldo Emerson wrote a poem titled 'Brahma'. So, I read it. This is how seepage happens—ideas and thoughts that migrate from one mind to another.

So, the next time you meet an elder, ask them a question or two. You might be surprised at their opinions; you will be enriched by their knowledge. You will be in their shoes one day.

93

Read Poetry and May Your Tribe Increase

'WHY DO YOU LIKE poetry so much?' I asked my father again this morning.

He sighed. 'Because we had to memorize poems like "Abou Ben Adhem",' he replied. It was a tangential answer, one that attempted to pry loose and give word to something tenuous, precious. My father began reciting the poem to deflect my tiresome questions. His voice was soft and a bit slurred, thanks to newly acquired dentures, I strained to hear him. '(…) like a lily in bloom (…) an angel writing in leaves of gold.'

My mouth opened with another question. My father started reciting again. 'Abou Ben Adhem, may his tribe increase.'

The first time I heard the phrase, 'May your tribe increase', was about five years ago from my friend, K. Srikrishna. He included it in a thank-you note that he sent after a party. I liked the phrase and started including it in my thank-you notes. It seemed like a quintessentially Indian expression.

'In India, we don't thank a person,' I told my husband grandly. 'We offer blessings, and that too, not to the individual—to the group. We don't take ownership of an action or even our spouse. Objects and actions belong to the community. We say "hum" (we), not "main" (I), not *my* husband but the husband. We don't say, I wish you well. We say, "May your tribe increase".'

'And it has,' the husband replied drily. 'To become the second most populous nation on earth.'

After my father recited the poem, I realized that the phrase I was making much of wasn't Indian at all. It came from a poem written by Leigh Hunt, a nineteenth-century English poet, who, it turns out, wrote about grasshoppers and crickets, death and fish.

My father is a worrywart. When my brother was commanding Very Large Crude Carriers (VLCCs), ships that plied the oceans, my dad worried that some drunk sailor would throw the captain—my brother—off the ship. My dad's worries came not from payments or promotions but his magnificent imagination. Poetry gives him solace, and turns his worries into structured chunks of lovely words or verses. He is a quiet man, my dad—doesn't talk much, except on topics he cares about. And these days, what he likes to talk about is poetry. No matter what the topic, he can link it to poetry.

'Appa, what shall I say about silence?' I once asked before speaking at a panel discussion.

'You can use Shakespeare's sonnets,' he replied and began reciting. 'When to the sessions of sweet silent thought, I summon up remembrances of things past [Sonnet 30].'

Poetry has become a hook, a way to converse with my dad. He loves English poetry and knows a hell of a lot about it. Shakespeare is his favourite, but he also loves the Romantic poets who lived in the Yorkshire moors in close proximity to each other. He talks about Ralph Waldo Emerson, Henry David Thoreau and T.S. Eliot when I ask about poets who had an Indian connection. In his poem, *The Waste Land*, Eliot talked about 'What the thunder said' and used the phrase, '*Datta, Dayadhvam, Damyata* (Give, Sympathize, Control).'

The Waste Land is a brilliant poem. There are strands of nonsensical phrases and lines in German, French, Italian and Sanskrit. It is a nightmare to memorize. But once it seeps in, I can imagine that it will change a person—which is the purpose of all art: to change how you view the world.

As my father's daughter, I wrestle with poetry. Prose seems more straightforward and less forced. Regional poetry in my native tongue, Tamil, or even translated Sanskrit, Spanish or Russian, sounds better to my novice ears. But perhaps I am approaching it all wrong. Poetry, like yoga, music, meditation or sports, is a practice, one that you get better at. Reading and memorizing poetry makes you see the world through a singular and distinctive lens. It shapes the way you see things, and you may well be eighty years old—like my dad—before you relish its rewards.

Is poetry relevant in today's world? The way to answer that question is to pick a poet, memorize their poems and see if they influence you. Do it often enough, and these poems may give you endurance, courage and joy. Ancient India has a long tradition of poetry in every language. The ones I follow are Sanskrit poets. *Bharatiya Kaavya Shastra*, they called it, and the list of luminaries is long: Bharata, Dandin, Udbatha, Vamana, Rudrata, Anandavardhana, Abhinavagupta, Rajashekara, Kunthaka, Dhananjaya, Bhoja, Kshemendra, Mamatta, Vishwanatha, Jagannatha and Kalidasa. No women. Thankfully, my native tongue, Tamil, has fine women poets—Andal and Avvaiyar being the ones I am most familiar with.

Poetry is a child of leisure. It takes a while to appreciate phrases like the 'wild braid of creation trembles' in Stanley Kunitz's 1933 masterpiece, *The Snakes of September*. How, then can you access poetry beyond simply memorizing as much as you can? Thankfully, we have options. *Mint Lounge* publishes poetry, as do Muse India, Poetry India, ReadLeafPoetry, Kritya.in, The (Great) Indian Poetry Collective and the Verseville (formerly the *Enchanting Verses Literary Review*), among others.

Delhi is the place to be. They have the Poets Corner group, Delhi Poetry Slam and the Delhi Poetry Festival—from 18 to 20 December at Siri Fort Auditorium; mark your calendars. Performance poetry à la Sarah Kay may be the future, or tweeting poems on X à la Kaafiya—The Poetry Festival. I don't know. I am not a poet, although I would like to be one.

94

Look at an Empty Space or Eternity

LOOK AT THIS PAGE, for example.
Take a breath.
That's it.

95

Describe Wine in Five Words or More

THE KILLER APP, AT least in the fields of wine, perfume, cheese or anything that relies on olfactory and gustatory sensations, will be able to transport scent and taste through cyberspace. If you could click on a wine bottle displayed on your computer and smell the aroma, all the wine descriptions we struggle to come up with would be rendered useless in an instant.

There are some things that words have trouble conveying. What Arthur Schopenhauer said about 'the inexpressible depth of music, so easy to understand and yet so inexplicable',[1] could well apply to the scent and taste of an aged Pinot Noir; complex fragrances, be it from Roja Dove, Tom Ford or Dior; unpasteurized cheeses; or to come back to Schopenhauer's quote, the sound of the children's choir at an old church in Goa at dusk. These are things that have to be experienced in person. When you try to convey the experience to someone who wasn't there, you grasp unsuccessfully at words.

As a species, we have gotten very good at describing what we see, but we haven't come up with the proper way to communicate things that we experience through our other senses. Music-streaming apps have simplified the audio part of it. If we want to share the ecstasy of listening to Mukhtiyar Ali's Sufi music with friends abroad, we simply send them a YouTube, SoundCloud or Spotify link; that hasn't happened to taste and smell. How do you convey the vibrant masculinity of a Barolo? Even saying this sounds pretentious and sexist.

This, then, is the conundrum for wine lovers: How do you convey the taste of a favourite wine to a friend who lives far away? For now, words, feeble as they are, will have to do. And they aren't doing their job well; witness the finger-pointing and controversy over wine terms.

The problem gets worse because words frame and manipulate the wine-drinking experience, as Baba Shiv, a professor of marketing at Stanford University's Graduate School of Business in the US, knows very well. Prof. Shiv has conducted numerous studies on how descriptions affect our experience of wine. In one famous study, he hooked subjects to an MRI machine and gave them some wine to drink (now that's a study I would like to participate in). When he told them that the wine was expensive, the pleasure receptors of the brain lit up. The subjects didn't merely think that they enjoyed the expensive wine more; their bodies and brains behaved as if they did.

To quote the paper, 'Our results show that increasing the price of a wine increases subjective reports of flavour pleasantness as well as blood-oxygen-level-dependent activity in the medial orbitofrontal cortex, an area that is widely thought to encode for experienced pleasantness during experiential tasks.' The next time you pour a friend a glass of red wine, tell her it is a Château Margaux. The simple statement will enhance her pleasure at having it.

How, then, should you describe wine? Two columnists have come up with solutions and written books in the process. *The Wall Street Journal*'s Lettie Teague, known for her no-nonsense approach to wine, says you need five words to describe all wines: acidity, aroma, balance, structure and texture. *Wine Spectator* columnist Matt Kramer says something similar but uses seven words: insight, harmony, texture, layers, finesse, surprise and nuance. While I love Teague's light-hearted columns, her words don't help me much. Neither do Kramer's. They are far too broad to be useful.

I have a few terms that I use to jog my scent and taste memory with respect to wines. Herbaceous (like Indian gooseberry or amla), jammy (best described by a Tamil phrase, kozha-kozha) and minerally (like drinking water from a copper pot), among others.

But 'minerally' too is a description that has come under attack. In an article published in the *Australian Journal of Grape and Wine Research* in June 2013, titled 'Exploring Minerality of Burgundy Chardonnay Wines', three scientists from the Université de Bourgogne in Dijon, France, studied how 'wine experts conceptualize minerality and explore whether they can judge wine minerality in a consensual way.' They concluded, 'Wine experts showed strong disagreement in their minerality judgements—'

So, if nobody agrees on anything, what are we to do? Are words superfluous in the wine universe? How can we convey the pleasures of a particular bottle of wine?

One sommelier, quoted in Bianca Bosker's 29 July 2015 article in *The New Yorker*, 'Is There A Better Way to Talk About Wine?', described a Barolo as tasting like a 'male ballet dancer'; a 'Baryshnikov in a glass', as Bosker says.

If you open this door, India has poetic descriptions to fit our wines. The proverbial Elizabeth aunty, whose home-made wines are famous throughout Kottayam, could describe a Malbec as having the 'balance and spikiness of very good Navara (or, more correctly, Njavara rice)'. Debashish Babu of Kolkata could describe a particular Cabernet Sauvignon as 'flabby—like the Brahmaputra in spate'. Or you could sip a Chenin blanc and say, 'Insipid, like Aunty Maria's pork vindaloo.'

We Indians have tasted wines for over 5,000 years. According to K.T. Acharya's *Indian Food: A Historical Companion,*[2] Sita promised to pour 1,000 jars of wine into the river Ganga in the hope of safe passage back when their exile ended. When they returned, Ram gave her maireya, a spiced wine (a ghastly concoction, according to me). Their entire city was reeling with drunken orgies. Presumably, a few citizens described the wines they tasted to their neighbours.

We need to explore our history, heritage and local vocabulary to describe wines in a way that resonates and makes sense to us. With its prodigious practice in the art of living, Goa would be a good place to start.

96

Use Your Cell Phone for Divination

When my mother bought a new Panchang calendar for 2019, I realized I had a better method because I used my smartphone not just to plan my days and weeks but also for divination. I don't mean that I used apps—tarot cards or fortune-telling ones—to predict the future. I used, and still use, the phone itself.

Divination operates under a simple but subtle premise: the universe is trying to send you messages if only you would learn to listen. Roman augurs used to look at the flight of birds every morning to decipher the will of the Gods. Persians used to open the Quran to a specific page to get signs from God (Fal-i-Quran). We can use our phones for these purposes.

Divination operates under a simple but subtle premise: the universe is trying to send you messages if only you would learn to listen.

My Hindu ancestors believed that if a bell rang after a statement, it would come true. The same could be said of trilling phones. The other day, a visiting friend made what I thought was an outrageous statement. Knowing my love of dancing, she said, 'You are going to be on stage with the best dance troupe in Bengaluru.' Nonsense, I thought. Her phone rang. My phone rang. 'Satyam (Truth),' we both chorused in unison, as our grandparents did when the bells rang after a random statement. Long story short. A top Kathak dance troupe asked me to be on stage with them, not to dance but to announce each dance.

I didn't always use my phone this way. In my earlier avatar, I was just another spaced-out smartphone user, filled with self-loathing about my phone addiction. Then, one day, and perhaps it was meant to be, I scrolled down my messages, skimming over the spam offerings of pest control, carpet cleaning and movie tickets, and saw one message with a discount code: 'love plants'. I don't know why I paid attention. I had a persistent cough. All the pills I was popping didn't help. Perhaps a herb would.

So, I clicked and went to the website that was advertising this discount. The first plant on the rotating banner of their homepage was an Indian herb that was good for cough. Was the universe talking to me? I ordered the herb; it came in a few days; I ingested its juice and felt better. Maybe my cough would have gone anyway. But the exercise made me pay attention to the rhythm and rhyme of messages that made their way into my phone.

Carl Jung and Nobel prize-winning physicist Wolfgang Pauli proposed that synchronicity operates on the principle that two seemingly unconnected incidents, upon deeper observation, are connected. Pauli said that numbers spoke to us.

I am not good with numbers. Perhaps because of that, it is easy for me to see them as symbols and designs. Consider an OTP I received today while trying to book an airline ticket: 210558. I don't know if you can see 21 as a water jug. Or if you can see the 558 as a train engine with two wheels. That is what I saw—and I stopped buying the airline ticket. I'll tell you why.

I was going from Bengaluru to Chennai for one day. There were two reasonably convenient options: a flight or the overnight train. I read the OTP numbers to signal that I should take the train. Using these 'signals' is easy when the stakes are low. I wish I could tell you something dramatic happened, but nothing did. I saved some money by taking the train, that's it.

The greater benefit when viewing your phone as an oracle is that it forces you to stop and tune in. For example, when I go on 'Find Friends' to check my daughter's whereabouts, her location on the map will remind me of a friend living there. Previously, I would have done nothing about it. These days, I call or text the long-lost friend, often surprised by the reaction: 'I was just thinking about you.' These days, I don't get irritated by spam messages. I glance at them like a gold-digger looking for a nugget.

Once you start doing this, it is incredible how quickly you learn and how self-perpetuating the cycle is. You listen to your phone and connect it to stuff happening in your world. You look for signs that can guide you. Best of all, you don't need to pick it up when you are bored or anxious.

You wait for the oracle inside your phone to call you.

97

Why Balance Wins

A RETIREMENT LETTER MASQUERADING as a wise sermon should hardly make news, let alone cause effusive gushing. Yet, in 2015, that happened with a letter written by Google's chief financial officer, Patrick Pichette. In it, Pichette announced that he was stepping down from his high-powered job and explained why. In terms of life lessons, little was new, but he put it well.

In the letter, he described standing atop Mount Kilimanjaro in Tanzania with his wife. After a few minutes spent staring at the Serengeti, his wife came up with a proposition: Why not keep travelling, she asked—from Africa to India to Bali to Australia to Antarctica? Pichette replied they had to go back to their jobs and board positions, at which point his wife asked when would it be their time? 'So when is it going to be time? Our time? My time. The questions just hung there in the cold morning African air,'[1] he wrote.

Pichette comes across as a nice man. He has a lyrical turn of phrase. That, and the fact that he held a top job in a revered Silicon Valley company may be why his resignation letter has the drama it does. Man rockets to the top, then chooses to drop off the cliff. That's the story. *The Washington Post* praised it as 'candid' and 'reflective'; the *HuffPost* called it 'inspiring'. Most people admired his desire to seek balance in his life.

However, prior to this point, Pichette had not sought work-life balance. The life he describes was no different from the hard-charging worker bees he managed—working long hours, travelling constantly, sometimes leaving the spouse to do much of the child-rearing, being available on call and email continually even when they did not need to be. When he found himself standing atop an African mountain with his wife, asking tough questions, he realized how much time had flown by; even the children had flown the coop. Stepping down from the post (CFO) and career at that juncture wasn't wisdom or a search for balance. It was exhaustion, giving way to spousal priorities. It was a simple resignation letter masquerading as a sermon from the mount.

What should make news are stories of those who choose balance on every step of the corporate ladder. Leaders who make career compromises for the sake of a gifted or dyslexic child; CFOs who choose to forgo more stock options so that they can be home on weekends; heads of divisions who take annual vacations sans the laptop with their families; law firm partners who forgo an exciting assignment so that their spouse can have a turn at the career wheel; and all those who don't need to get on a mountain top to understand work-life balance. Except those people probably don't become Google CFOs and get its bully pulpit.

Balance in today's world is mostly about saying 'No'. Pichette stepped off his ostensibly fabulous job when he resigned, which is why he is lauded. For the rest of us, it is a series of small negative shakes of the head. A list of things not to do. Small things, but hard to implement. How addicted are you to your mobile device? How much time do you spend checking your messages and email? I do it constantly. Every study says that this frazzled, constant checking of digital data fries your creativity and drowns your concentration. How do you switch off? Are you doing anything about it? That is balance.

Do you surreptitiously check messages when you are helping your child with homework? Why? How can you stop yourself? Parenting happens during pauses, during boredom. Sometimes, it is just being at the right place when your child has a certain question. It is the ability to pick up on cues and know what questions to ask. To do that, you cannot be preoccupied all the time. How will you achieve a free, open mind that picks up on cues from people you care about? That is balance.

Pichette says he is leaving Google to travel the world with his wife. How about going to the corner store with her? Grand gestures make for good storytelling, but the small stuff makes a marriage. Date night is a Western concept, but doing something with your spouse is a good idea. People of our parents' generation didn't make a conscious effort to do an activity together, but we can.

Balance is about saying no to trips you don't need to take to come up with alternatives such as teleconferencing. Balance is walking away from an assignment that you really love to help a friend get through his illness. Balance is small, incremental choices in a direction that is fair to all the people you care about; that encompasses the physical, mental and spiritual, that incorporates hobbies, passion and purpose. It is not about standing on a mountain and announcing that you are dropping out. That is drama, not balance.

Balance means having priorities beyond immediate family (spouse and children) and your career. Our Indian system is geared for balance. You need to have things to prioritize family, friends, duty and obligations; these are the stuff of balance. India is full of that. A family wedding falls on the same day as a product roadshow. Which do you choose? A Silicon Valley CFO probably never used the line, 'My second cousin's wedding is on the day of the launch. We grew up together, and I have to attend—for four days.'

India is rigged for a balanced life. We each have elderly relatives for whom we are sort of responsible. We don't necessarily like these aunties and uncles, but a cousin calls from Europe and says they need to be taken for a blood test. What do you do? Having multiple people and obligations in our lives gives us perspective and prevents us from being consumed by one thing: our career.

If you don't have college classmates who will nudge you to take a trip every year, how will you know the pleasure of friendship or, for that matter, vacations? If you don't go to church regularly, or have some sort of spiritual affiliation, how do you pause to think about the big things in life? If you don't look up from your computer to watch a sunset, how will you get a hobby that will engage you after retirement? If you don't find pleasure in art, gardening, nature or sport, how will you prepare yourself for the solitude accompanying old age?

Balancing involves choosing between conflicting priorities. For many, there is no conflict. The priority becomes work. To me, Pichette's letter isn't an inspiring take on balance. It is an extended apology for all the small things he didn't say 'No' to. Because, you see, balance isn't sequential; it is parallel—and constant.

98

What Verbal Personality Type Are You?

WHAT IS YOUR VERBAL tic? Do you say 'like' or 'means' more than twice in a sentence? Big data has discovered that men say 'uh', and women say 'um', according to *The Atlantic* magazine.[1] Perhaps yours is not so much a verbal tone as that conveying the wrong impression. You are not a complainer, but you have a whiny voice. You think you are flexible, but your tone is clipped, giving the impression of rigidity.

I have a verbal tone that drives my husband nuts. It is needlessly tentative. 'Why do your sentences trail off towards the end?' he will ask. 'Why do you ask questions instead of just stating facts, especially since these are subjects you know?'

I think I speak this way because … wait, scratch that. Let me be declarative, and you will see why. I adopted this tone from childhood habits. I was taught to speak a certain way to avoid appearing arrogant.

Our speech patterns are deeply ingrained, and most of us don't know how or why we speak the way we do. Some of it is because we mimic the speech of those we admire. Some of it is because of our inner biases playing out in the cadence of our speech, and some of it has to do with assertiveness.

Do you declare ('This research paper is hogwash'), or do you hedge ('Seems to me and I could be wrong, but this research paper doesn't read quite right')?

Do you speak forcefully ('India wants an answer') or do you speak softly ('Don't mean to push, but would you like to answer that?')

Assertive people speak to claim attention. Reticent types speak to connect. Speech patterns also have to do with whether you are comfortable with disagreement. Some of us hate confrontation. We don't interrupt others and fall silent when we are interrupted. Arnab Goswami would render such people practically mute. Both men and women interrupt a woman four times more than they would interrupt a man.

The problem arises when your speech doesn't reflect who you are. You may be confident, but your speech is tentative. You may second-guess yourself to be polite but appear unsure of your opinion ('I may be wrong, but I think XYZ has some issues'). Do you have speech patterns that you have fallen into, and which you need to outgrow? Do you qualify your statements, and if so, why? To appear nice? ('You probably know this already, but everything is relative, isn't it?')

Assertive folk speak two-and-a-half times more than the shy, retiring types in classrooms, meetings and boardrooms. When someone interrupts the shy retiring types, they shut up, and take a while to speak up again. They are vulnerable to interruption, as the jargon goes.

This applies in social settings as well. A few people jump in assertively during a debate or a discussion at a party or salon. They interrupt each other constantly. When things get heated, they have no problem out-shouting each other. They think fast on their feet and state opinions authoritatively, even if they are wrong.

The other group waits to be heard. They engage in 'turn-taking' behaviour. They don't interrupt; if they do, they aren't loud enough. They wait to formulate perfect opinions before they open their mouths. They worry about being seen (and judged) as stupid or ill-informed. Predictably, women speak far less in public than men. One-on-one, it is the opposite.

The next time you are at a lecture and the speaker invites people to ask questions, notice the ratio of men to women. Which gender asks more questions? The question is what to do with this information. If you are running a meeting, or convening a business conclave where men outnumber women 3:1, as they usually do, what is your approach?

If you want to make sure that the shy brainy folk contribute to the meeting, what is a good strategy?

One approach would be to simply pause. Take a moment before responding to what someone has said. Be aware of how you are responding to women versus men; Microsoft CEO Satya Nadella discovered that too late.

Notice your biases and body language. Are you choosing men to answer 'impactful' questions and tossing the lighter questions to women? The idea is to cultivate a memory for your behaviour and biases to make your responses seem equitable.

Society lays the onus on women. 'Lean in,' says Facebook Chief Operating Officer (COO) Sheryl Sandberg. Break the glass ceiling.

Speak up. Dance like a man. That is one way.

If you are the boss, tell your quiet colleagues to speak up. Or you can simply hire more women.

As has been reported in *The New York Times*, *Harvard Business Review*, *Inc.* and *The Atlantic*, teams with more women outperformed teams with more men on a consistent basis. 'The Secret to Smart Groups: It's Women' a headline in *The Atlantic* said. [2]

99
Doodle

USE THIS EMPTY PAGE to doodle. And see how it relaxes you. Then continue doodling during long meetings to calm down.

100

Embrace Dualism

WHERE DO COOL IDEAS come from? Every year, the online salon edge.org poses one question and gets many smart people to answer it. The 2011 question was: What scientific concept would improve everybody's cognitive toolkit? The answers, compiled in a book with the laughably ambitious title, *This Will Make You Smarter: New Scientific Concepts to Improve Your Thinking*, has 165 contributions from eminent thinkers on varied subjects: anthropophilic, cognitive humility, haecceity (or quiddity; which means the property of being a unique and individual thing) and other such abstruse concepts.[1]

Some themes emerge out of this morass of ideas. One that informs this column is called dualism.

Although the word immediately connotes spirituality and philosophy, dualism in this context has little to do with Dvaita or Descartes (Cartesian dualism is the philosophical view that the mind [*res cogitans*] and the body [*res extensa*] are distinct and separate substances). Instead, it has its genesis in quantum theory and wave-particle duality.

Just as matter is both, wave-like and particle-like, why can't the same idea represent two opposing truths, ask the essayists? Ergo dualism: the notion that two opposite realities can express one underlying truth is a bit mind-bending, but don't give up. As you will see, dualism comes naturally to us.

Indians are adept at holding two contradictory thoughts in their heads. We are a surging economy, yet our streets are filled with beggars. We have the fourth highest number of global dollar-billionaires, yet we fall deep down the world poverty index. Every tourist photo shows Indians smiling like they mean it, yet we are not one of the happiest places on the planet. Even commonplace sights on our streets are rife with duality or two realities. Cows stand or sit beside road dividers, yet they don't get run over; the traffic weaves around them. Vendors who sell us fruits, vegetables and coconut water are both crafty and honest in their way. Extended families are both a pain and a pleasure, depending on the mood and the moment just like our food both sweet and sour.

In this age of specialization, dualism presents a powerful alternative. To hold two contradictory ideas in your head implies a certain comfort with ambiguity, the grey zone. Children have the ability to hold not just two contradictory thoughts but multiple such thoughts in their heads at the same time. We call it imagination.

Dualism represents a stark contrast to the dichotomy that percolates our cultural conversation these days. Embracing the physicist's meaning of duality, writer Amanda Gefter says:

> [...] could serve as a potent antidote to our typically Boolean, two-valued, zero-sum thinking—where statements are either true or false, answers are yes or no, and if I'm right, then you are wrong. With duality, there's a third option. Perhaps my argument is right and yours is wrong; perhaps your argument is right and mine is wrong; or, just maybe, our opposing arguments are dual to one another.[2]

Dualism is not just about quantum theory or world-changing ideas. It works in smaller contexts, too. The next time you have an argument with your spouse or partner, maybe you can take the high road by preaching dualism.

She may be convinced she is right, and you know you are right. Guess what? You both may be right. That's dualism. Wrap your head around that concept.

As India grows from a service economy to an entrepreneurial one, I would like to submit that we capitalize on our natural inclination towards dualism and turn it into a potent wellspring for innovative ideas.

Where do cool ideas come from? Some, like Flipkart, are adapted from ideas that work. Some, like the boys on Chowpatty Beach who will spread a mat on the sand and get your chaat order from the crowded stalls nearby, come from spotting a need and addressing it. Some, like the Nano, come from an engineering mindset of tinkering and improving. But true Einsteinian, Jobs-like innovation comes from none of these places. It comes from your solar plexus, from your gut, from your soul. It comes from that frisson of fear and excitement as you stand at the crossroads of an unknown place and realize that every notion you held as dear and true could be overturned in your head through a radical idea that came out of nowhere. That's when you hug yourself with joy and nervousness. That's when you call the private equity guys.

101

Gargle and Swirl after Eating

ONE OF THE THINGS that Indian kids are often told to do is gargle and swirl water in their mouths after eating. In Tamil, we call it 'koppilichu', although I am sure there are different names in each Indian language. We eat with our hands. When we wash our hands after the meal, we are told to wash our mouth with water.

Along the same lines, consider doing this gargle-and-swirl every time you drink water. Occasionally, just gargle. Gargling is good for the mouth. If you are alone in front of the office water cooler, take a sip of water, throw your head back and gargle loudly. It will help your throat. The only problem is if your boss walks by and sees you gurgling like a baby.

Facial exercises such as opening your mouth wide into a simhasana (lion pose) can work on your facial muscles and prevent them from sagging. The only problem is that these need to be done consistently and long-term. If you need an instant jolt of beauty, consider all the new treatments with long words, such as micro-dermabrasion, vitamin C serum, hyaluronic acid and others.

Ayurveda prescribes gargling for a variety of ills, including, the cough. It also has specific decoctions for gargling linked to your illness and constitution. Even if you don't go to that extent, simply using warm water to gargle will improve your vocal tone and oral cavity.

102

Be Vulnerable

EVEN THOUGH HE WAS over the top and occasionally overwrought in his performances, we each have our favourite Robin Williams movies. Whether it was the charismatic professor of *Dead Poets Society* (1989), the divorced husband who dressed up as a housekeeper in *Mrs. Doubtfire* (1993), or the suburban dad leading his family on vacation in *Runaway Vacation* (2006), Williams' magnetic presence often eclipsed his co-stars.

To each role, he brought great comic timing and voice modulation. But what made him an icon, in my view, was his frequent and honest displays of vulnerability: the trembling lips, the crazed eyes that revealed inner demons we knew not which, the ironic half-smile which said, 'You don't know the half of it (of what goes on in my head).'

Williams took not just his inner demons but our vulnerabilities and insecurities as well and portrayed them in full technicolour. The only other actor who came close was Nathan Lane, his co-star in my all-time favourite movie, *The Birdcage* (1996). I know its dialogues by heart.

If you haven't seen it, you must watch it not only for its beautiful South Beach setting and funny storyline but for the three actors at the top of their game: Robin Williams, Nathan Lane and Gene Hackman. It is one of the few movies in which Williams plays it down and lets Lane and Hackman vie for screen domination. It is perhaps why I love this movie: frailties on display for all to see; frailties that mirror our own and make us nod in recognition.

Not all good actors do this well. Leonardo DiCaprio has grown into a magnificent actor, but vulnerability is not what he's about. Neither is

Tom Hanks, Russell Crowe or the late great Philip Seymour Hoffman. To portray vulnerability, you have to be fearless. You must confront your demons and leave them out to dry; display them for all to see. You have to have enough courage or heartbreak to tie a belt around your neck and hang yourself. RIP Robin Williams.

Vulnerability is a topic that made social psychologist Brené Brown famous. In November 2006, Texas-based Brown sent her husband and children to her in-laws for the weekend. She spread out 11,000 pieces of qualitative data (interviews with people) that she had collected over six years of research all over her house, asking questions to which she had no answer: Why do some people live wholeheartedly while others don't? Why do some people believe they are worthy of love while others don't?

As she sifted through the exhaustive interviews she had done over the years, Brown had an epiphany. It resulted in a TED talk that has had over sixteen million views and counting and is the fourth most-watched TED talk of all time.

At her Texas home, Brown made two lists: the 'bad' list and the 'wholehearted' list. Wholehearted people lived fearlessly. They took risks without fear of rejection. Brown assumed that they lived differently because they came from better circumstances. This, it turned out, was not true. Wholehearted people, too, had experienced trauma. They came from broken homes and divorced families, and faced addiction and other ills. Yet they lived differently. They embraced life rather than shrinking from it. 'Why?' asked Brown. The reason had to do with character.

The people in Brown's 'bad' list had certain traits that caused them to live differently. They were perfectionists, judgmental, wore busyness as a status symbol, valued productivity, wanted to prove their superiority, didn't get emotional and viewed emotion as a bad thing. They were top performers who worried about what other people thought. They liked certainty, and wanted to do it all—do it perfectly and make it appear effortless.

Recognize yourself? 'How can we embrace rest and play if we have tied our self-worth to what we produce?' asks Brown in a TED talk.

'In order to be wholehearted, you have to allow yourself to be broken-hearted.'[1] You have to allow yourself, as Williams did, to be vulnerable. Or you have to die trying.

Countless students have just started their first year of college, in India or abroad, at JIPMER or IITs, NID or LSR.[2] They will be confronting students who are brilliant and competitive. They will measure themselves against their peers and come up short. Some students—like the 2014 Fields Medal winners Artur Avila, Martin Hairer, Manjul Bhargava and Maryam Mirzakhani—will be so superior to their peers in intellect that they will do all the academics and do it effortlessly. But what if you are average? What if you are sincere in intent, competent in execution and kind as a human? Is that enough? How do you measure yourself in this hyper-competitive world where all the qualities Brown listed are valued?

One option would be to get off the treadmill. The other, a more realistic option, especially if you are eighteen and a first-year college student, is to face up to your strengths and weaknesses—that requires the kind of courage that came effortlessly to Robin Williams. But for the rest of us who wear the carapace of infallibility as armour, it requires effort and a very specific sort of cultivation.

103

Consider a Smidgeon of Fear

CONSIDER BACK FLIPS. I attempted this in my building's pool. After watching all the children do this routinely, to the point where they looked like somersaulting jellyfish, I decided to give it a try. It's harder than you think, particularly if you learn it as an adult. I swim well. But it is one thing to plunge forward into the deep end or dive face first. It is quite another to fall backwards. So, I stand at the deep end and listen to a little child yell at me to put my head back and down into the water. I can't do it. Fear of falling, fear of drowning overcomes all my rational thoughts that I cannot drown in a swimming pool. I throw my head back, attempt a yogic chakrasana pose under water, and flip out. I come out gasping. Why do I persist? I hate this exercise. It is the foolish belief that out of this smidgen of fear will arise an expanse of the possibility of what I can do. This is why people run marathons after age 60, or climb Mount Everest without oxygen tanks.

So, what is your crucible of fear? If you don't have any, let me give you suggestions to explore: spiders, the fear that your pink Pantacid will explode into a monster, the fear that a ghost will whack you from behind when you walk on a dimly-lit road alone at night. Or how much the fear that an earthworm will escape from the apple you just ate and gobble up your intestine? Whatever your fear is, explore it, just a smidgeon.

104

Play Ancient Board Games

IT IS A SIMPLE game involving five medium-sized pebbles. We called it Five Stones or Seven Stones, but it could well have been played with any odd number of stones. It took a little practice, and there was room for improvement. You started by throwing one pebble up in the air and picked up another pebble while it fell. Then you graduated by picking up two pebbles while one was in the air, then three and more. You could throw two pebbles in the air and attempt to pick up an equal number. It took concentration and hand-eye coordination. It absorbed my friends and me for hours when we were children.

We often played it on hot summer afternoons at my grandmother's house when the adults slept. But the game, which required little more than a flat surface and five stones, could be played in railway compartments, waiting rooms and balconies. We spent much time foraging for the right-sized pebbles and cowrie shells to add to the game's toolkit.

An excellent website called Traditionalgames.in has a video clip showing how the game is played. Other websites devoted to traditional games conjecture that this simple game spread through the Silk Route to Turkey, Spain and Korea, where it is called Besh Dash, Payana and Gonggi, respectively. Having played it for years, I can attest that it does indeed improve eyesight, concentration and motor skills. In fact, I have restarted playing it because it—like doodling—is a great stress buster and a harbinger of the elusive muse that only surfaces when you are distracted or in a Zen state of mind.

India is home to many of the world's most ancient games, including Pachisi, which was exported to England, recreated into Ludo, and then returned to India to be played by many a child during the summer holidays. 'Nowadays, Indian children play Ludo completely oblivious to the fact that it is a monstrous decomposition of their own fantastic board game,' said Irving Finkel in *Time* magazine in 2008. Finkel, who works at The British Museum, is an authority on board games, including the Royal Game of Ur, widely considered the oldest board game.

India's contribution to board games is extensive, as documented by experts like Finkel, R. Vasantha and V. Balambal. In speeches and reports, Vasantha describes some of the more interesting indoor games, such as Mancala, Tigers and Goats, and Single Track. Balambal, who specializes in the indoor games of Tamil Nadu, is mentioned in Levingston's Board Game Blog.[1] She also finds mention in a hard-to-find book called *Sedentary Games of India*, edited by Nirbed Ray and Amitabha Ghosh. Anyone interested in how board games were created, spread and played should read these blogs.

My favourite game used to be Snakes and Ladders, but now I find that it too is a monstrous translation of the original Indian version. In 1860, a Harvard dropout named Milton Bradley created a board game called The Checkered Game of Life, or Life, as it was popularly called. In the game, the players simulated their travels through life with jobs, children, education and hurdles. The Game of Life was arguably America's first parlour game and certainly its most popular.

Bradley may have popularized the game, but he borrowed its ideas from many an ancient culture, including India, where this checkerboard and the accompanying game were called by various names: Jnana Chaupar, Gyan Chaupar and Parama Pada Sopanam (steps to the highest place). Originating around 1200 CE in India, this game had squares called houses and four players whose movements were dictated by the throw of dice. It was thought to be excellent preparation for the victories and vicissitudes of life, with all its glorious vagaries.

Players took on personas, and if they were virtuous, they climbed the ladder. Fortunes changed with the throw of a dice, which brought along winds of change. If you were unlucky, you were swallowed by a snake and had to go down several steps. But don't fear, was the underlying message: After every snake came a ladder; after falling, you would go up.

The main thing was to maintain equanimity because the game had no clear winner. All that mattered was reaching the top of the board; and eventually, every player would. The original game didn't have the 'winner-take-all' strategy that became part of its Western avatar. Rather, it was heavily imbued with the Hindu notion of *maya* or illusion that translated into ladders of success and snakes of failure, both of which were part of the game of life.

Traditional Indian games are being revived through companies such as Chennai-based Kreeda, Mysore-based Kreedaa Kaushalya and others.

I became interested in ancient Indian board games after listening to Jill Lepore's excellent lecture on 'The Meaning of Life' about Jnana Chaupar (also called Snakes and Ladders).

Say you are an elementary schoolteacher, and you want to teach your students the meaning of life with all its ups and downs; what do you do? Perhaps you should play Snakes and Ladders with them, not the modern version but the original Indian version.

And the next time you feel the urge to play a video game to take a break from your computer, why not collect five pebbles from your garden? Throwing and catching pebbles will distract you and soothe your tired eyes.

105
Call Your Mother

WHAT DO YOU DO when you need a recipe? Do you leaf through a recipe book, look online, or call your mother or mother-in-law? I got some young green peppercorns from Wayanad district, Kerala. You know the kind? They look like a cross between a string of pearls and an emerald. They taste like a bite after a particularly pungent quarrel.

You can eat green peppercorns raw, but mostly, they are pickled in brine. Nothing fancy—just some lemon juice and salt. The combination of tart lemon, salt and pungent pepper tastes of the tropics and is Zen in the simplicity of its ingredients. I ate these vine-ripened peppercorns during summer vacations in Kerala, where—short of marinating an annoying uncle—they cure fish, treat allergies and alleviate colds. Now that I had a basketful of young green peppercorns, I wanted the recipe to duplicate the taste of my childhood. So naturally, I did what all young women do when they need a recipe: I went on the Internet.

I looked at cookery YouTube videos, which are hard to do source at work. So, I prefer images and text that I can scroll through at speed. There is one nifty shortcut to recipes: Go to the images section of the search engine. Then type in the recipe name, and you'll get dozens of images of your favourite dish, whether you are making quesadillas, lamb kebabs, dum biryani or lemon rasam. Hone in on the photo of the dish that appeals to you and take it from there. You'll have to see if the proportions of the dish described match your household tolerance. Jain households might ruthlessly dismiss dishes that use garlic as a cover-up for flavour. Minimalist cooks may veer towards dishes with five or fewer ingredients. Cooks have quirks.

After browsing through the meagre offerings for pickled peppercorns, I realized how much my recipe hunting had changed. A decade ago, I have called, from all continents, aunties and occasionally, uncles, for recipes and advice about dishes. Why wasn't I doing this now? And what was I losing in the process?

Determined to rectify this lapse, I immediately picked up the phone and called my aunt in Kottayam. 'Do you remember those giant vats of green peppercorn pickle we used to devour in Vaikom?' I asked. 'What's the recipe for that?'

'Can you call me after three hours?' she replied. 'I am watching my television serials.' Was this why I had stopped calling her for recipes? Because she was held hostage to television serial schedules?

I called an old friend—known far and wide amongst his friends for his abhorrence of television, let alone serials. When I asked him for recipes with green peppercorns, he asked me to find a good match for his son, Rustom. We spent a pleasant half-hour talking about the travails of matchmaking for 'today's young people'. In between, he handed down some recipes I could not use because I am vegetarian.

One of his favourites was a chicken fry with green peppercorns. 'Try this with tofu,' he said helpfully), which I had seen on 'Nandinisfood.com'. But Nandini's food did not have memories, anecdotes and fears of a son being gay, mixed in with the recipes. Along the way, my friend bandied about his entirely made-up but plausible-sounding theories: Moroccan tagine pots evolved from the mud pots used in Indian villages to cook over an open fire. Sounds good but so patently false. That's like saying eggs evolved from oranges because they are both round. Well, eggs perhaps did—evolve from oranges, but only over many millennia and mutations. By the end of our conversation, I still did not have my peppercorn recipe, but we came up with several potential matches for Rustom.

This is what we miss when we depend on the Internet or books for our recipes. The specificity of what they offer is great for someone short on time. But calling up family and friends for recipes is like the serendipitous browsing that happens when you open a dictionary. You search for the meaning of a word and discover several unknown new ones beside it.

The meandering storytelling of a recipe—along with offering directions in a unique way and brushing our teeth with neem twigs—is one of India's great oral traditions, passed down from generation to generation. You call someone up for a recipe and get kitchen tips, anecdotes, a slice of life, a touch of wisdom and an update on television serials.

For cooking crises, the Internet simply doesn't work. What do you do when you have put too much salt into a dal? Try googling that. Or call your mother, and she will tell you to throw in a slice of potato that will absorb the salt.

Next time you want a recipe, consider not opening your cookbook or searching for it online. Call up the aunt that you haven't spoken to for months, and you may be pleasantly surprised by the conversation that follows. She will be delighted to hear from you. Then, write it all down in a dog-eared notebook, complete with nonsensical footnotes that only you will understand. Save this notebook and pass it on to the next generation.

106

Don't Be Deaf to Your Body

MY MOTHER ALWAYS SAYS, 'Listen to your body.' Believe me, I have tried. I have sat quietly in the corner and tried to listen to my body. Beyond the rumbling of my stomach and an intense irrational craving for samosa, malpua or kulfi, I couldn't feel or hear anything. My body wasn't speaking to me.

What does the phrase, 'Listen to your body' even mean? Which part of your body do you listen to? Are you listening for sounds from your heart, stomach or intestines? Or are you paying attention to the aches and pains you feel? Finally, in desperation, I did something my Mom longed for: I asked her for help. I asked her a question.

There comes a time—perhaps when you are in your twenties or thirties—when you reach the conclusion that you know more than your parents. That is the stage of life when you stop asking your parents any meaningful questions. You still ask them random things: the name of that obscure uncle who disappeared in the Himalayas, the recipe for a particular spice mix made only in your family, and whether you really need to attend yet another christening, birth or death ceremony.

Beyond that, you mostly act as if your parents have reached their expiration date in the knowledge-transfer area This is exacerbated when the elders take to smartphones and telephone you while you are in the middle of a meeting, with questions like, 'What do I press to make this message go away?'

Every time my mother felt under the weather, she would not go to the doctor or even take medicine. She would say things like, 'The heat in my body has increased, which is why my eyes are dry. I think

I'm going to make a soup out of cooling green moong beans. Or drink some tender coconut water.'

When she had an upset stomach, she wouldn't pop a pink antacid. Instead, her remedy for her woes would depend on what her body was telling her. In some instances, she would starve herself till her stomach felt better. In others, she would drink a dark decoction made of tulsi (holy basil), cumin, green pepper and other herbs from the garden. And sometimes, she would put her feet into a bucket of warm water with some Epsom salt in good measure to take out 'all the toxins and negativities' from her body. She had specific reasons for these behaviours. But the underlying thread was the simple phrase: listen to your body.

One day, I went to her and said, 'Ma, what do you mean by listening to your body?' My mother looked overjoyed. First, she proceeded to feed me till saturation and then explosion-point, like all Indian mothers do. Then she sat me down and gave me a long lecture. I will spare you the details, but the gist is: don't assume that the external world can cure your internal problems. Sometimes, or rather, every time, according to my mother, your body will give you clues about its current state and where it is headed. Once you started paying attention, you will notice patterns and trends.

Physicians do this all the time. They ask the patient questions, make notes and form a diagnosis. But like my Mom said, no physician knows your body as well as you do. The only difference is that you don't pay attention to what your body is telling you, but a physician is trained to.

If it doesn't comes naturally to you, one way to incorporate this behaviour is to pretend to be your own physician and ask questions like, 'Why are you having this headache? Is it because you skipped a meal? Is it because you went out in the sun for too long?' 'Can you cure your headache by lying in a cold room for some time or by eating some healthy, hearty, warm soup?' Why not try different things and see what works?

Some of it is just experimentation. If you have a stomach ache, trace it back to its origin. Was it because of the food you ate last night? Or was it because you went out for a quick roadside snack that might have been unhygienically prepared?

Listening to your body becomes an art when you start taking stock every day, and if possible, several times a day. I am trying to do this. These days, after every meal, I try to pay attention to how I feel. I figure out if what I have eaten makes me feel good or bloated. Rather than get drowned in work and eat reflexively while watching a video, I try to pause and pay attention if I am feeling hungry. If I am, I eat something—maybe a few walnuts or a quick banana. I try to monitor my body using a few basic paradigms. Am I feeling hot or cold? Am I feeling dry or wet with a runny nose? Am I feeling gaseous or nauseous after I eat something? If my body aches, I stand up and stretch a little.

Being in tune with my body has many benefits. I can prevent minor illnesses before they show up. When I feel a cold coming on, I can pummel it with a host of home remedies, including ginger tea and steaming. I am slowly figuring out foods that agree with my body, and even though I am not at the 'I won't eat cabbage because it makes me feel gaseous,' I am getting there. Best of all, I have finally understood what listening to your body means, and my mother is delighted.

Of course, I don't listen to it all the time because it veers towards the healthy me. I like the unhealthy me enough to down a packet of Pringles, which taste like paper only because they were forbidden in my childhood, which, when you think about it, is the root of all our unhealthy eating habits: because our parents forbade them in our childhood.

So, if you are a parent, consider letting your babies self-feed. They may make a mess at first, but they will learn to eat what their bodies tell them to and stop when full.

107

Walk, Don't Drive, to Buy Fruits

As I WRITE THIS, I am slurping on watermelons. They are all over Bengaluru: glorious, green round balls with dark green veins piled a block high in Cox Town, near where I live. Chop them open for translucent flesh the colour of nail polish, pockmarked with pits that children spit while imagining whole orchards sprouting around them. The grapes are here, too. Fruit vendors roll carts piled high with that single fruit—one harvest's bounty.

Summer will soon be here—the relentless march of grapes, melons and watermelons, all culminating in the marvellous swansong that is the Indian mango. In two months, we will see mounds of golden mangoes—one variety after another till the scorching summer ends. I wait for the Imam Pasand and think Alphonso is overrated, but your opinion is welcome too.

Years ago, I interviewed the iconic chef Alice Waters about her cooking philosophy at Chez Panisse, California. Waters, who revolutionized American chefs' cooking, said simplicity and seasonality were her bywords. This same word—seasonal—was repeated by uber-chefs such as Daniel Boulud, Mario Batali, Jean-Georges Vongerichten and Thomas Keller. At the time, I didn't understand this word or the concept. Why was a seasonal menu so important to them? What did it even mean in the US, where you could buy luscious mangoes imported from Mexico at the Korean deli down the street in the dead of winter? Wasn't luxury the ability to eat anything anywhere, anytime?

We do this in urban India all the time now. We buy grapes from Chile, dragon fruit from Vietnam, melons from Bukhara and oranges from Malta throughout the year. The good news is that this overused foodie word can become your ally in India in the way our fruit and vegetable harvests play out. Simply put, 'seasonal' is what you cannot have.

In today's Bengaluru, you cannot have chikoos for love or money. Well, you can if you go to gourmet supermarkets, but should you? Papayas, too, are waning, as are pomegranates and oranges. You still get them, but they aren't ubiquitous. The humble mosambi (sweet lime) is coming into season, while loose-jacket oranges are slowly going off. Grapes are in their prime now and will last a week, tops, before the watermelons have their aria.

This specificity is the luxury of seasonal fruits and vegetables. It has to do with taste, time and geography. To eat a cauliflower in Delhi in the winter is to experience this vegetable in its prime. Certain fruits and vegetables are delicacies that make their appearance like shy heroines at the behest of nature and climate. Macrobiotics formalized these concepts by suggesting that people ought to eat only those foods that were indigenous, local and seasonal for health reasons.

Perhaps because of norms such as these, seasonality is a concept that was understood instinctively by people of the previous generation, regardless of country. Americans who grew up in the Depression Era of the 1930s understood the concept of seasonality because they were used to forgoing certain types of food.

Even today, Indians understand seasonality and how it is linked with taste and cost. Fresh figs will arrive in Delhi at certain times of the year, and it is best to devour them before they disappear. Strawberries from Panchgani and Mahabaleshwar will arrive in Mumbai, drawing envy from south Indians like me. Mumbaikars will devour them, and soon they'll be gone.

Among the Rajputs of Rajasthan, seasonality is interpreted as eating the choicest game at the perfect time. Ducks are most flavourful after they migrate from Siberia. Foie gras is eaten before the geese migrate back because their livers triple in size in preparation for the trip. Venison tastes best in spring because the four-horned deer, famous for its saddle meat, would have eaten fresh berries and fruits, lending its meat a lovely tartness by then. And most of Rajasthan will not eat meat in the monsoon or during the breeding season.

This interplay between feasting and fasting is the essence of living seasonally. The good news is that it is easily done in India. Instead of driving to the gourmet food store, all you need to do is buy in your local market.

108

Eat like Our Elders Did

WHEN MY CHINESE ROOMMATE got acne on her face, she ate a porridge made of green mung beans. Soaked mung beans are considered cooling foods in traditional Chinese medicine. They support the yin earth and disperse yang heat. Indian Ayurveda, too, has its own theories of heating and cooling foods. Ripe yellow mangoes are considered heating. My grandmother always ate mangoes with yoghurt to balance the fruit's intrinsic heat.

The mango theory didn't make sense to me, I told my Dad. Nature, after all, doesn't make mistakes. If it bestowed a bounty of mangoes all through the summer months, the fruits had to be there for a reason: to cool us off. No, said my Dad. Mangoes were indeed heating fruits; nature didn't make mistakes. The reason mangoes came to us in the summer was answered in a pithy Sanskrit saying, *Ushnam Ushnena Shamyati*, akin to the Latin *Similia Similibus Curantur*. Like cures like, in plain English. Thus, heating fruits like mangoes helps dispel the heat of summer.

Heating foods are a complicated business. Mangoes are heating, but only the ripe ones. Green mangoes are cooling—witness their ubiquitous usage in summer sherbets, including the famous aam panna, which incidentally includes some cooling cardamom, should there be any residual heat in the mangoes.

Yogurt is cooling and damp. Many elderly Indians will not eat yogurt at night because it causes kapha or mucus. A better option is buttermilk, particularly blended with heating spices such as ginger, pepper, curry leaves and asafoetida. This chhaas, or sambaaram as it is called in Kerala, is a soothing digestive. Sugarcane, which thrives in the summer, is heating, so you balance it with some cooling rock sugar or kalkandu.

Panakam is another traditional yet healthy drink made with jaggery, pepper, dried ginger and cardamom, it balances electrolytes and quenches thirst. The bael (Bengal quince) fruit is famously cooling. Starting in early summer, bael sherbets are sold in by-lanes all over India. The green fruits, about the size of a small football, will be stacked like a pyramid. The yellow insides will be scooped out, made into a pulp and served with spices and sugar.

Among the elders in my family, it was traditional to eat agasti leaves or agathi keerai (Sesbania grandiflora) on the twelfth lunar day or Dwadasi—after the previous day's Ekadasi fast—because it had vermicidal qualities. If that sounds like you are potting a plant, it is the opposite. You'd fast on Ekadasi day, and detox the following day. These days, we go to Ananda in the Himalayas, Uttarakhand or Canyon Ranch in the US to achieve the same effect.

Eat seasonal; according to tradition, like our elders do. They eat light.

Acknowledgements

MUCH OF THE MATERIAL came out of my mind, rife as it is with fears and foibles. I have thought about this stuff for years. I collect self-help columns and books, ingest them, use them and try variations. I try to compress them into easy-to-do-and-digest methods. I think in spurts, contradictions and shortcuts. I obsess over certain topics, specifically about how to game life and get rid of my addictions. As my kids say, 'It is exhausting.'

I live for teachable moments even though my children loathe them. So, in the end, this book is one long teachable moment for a silent audience, which if you want to know, is the stuff that my sweet dreams are made of.

So, I acknowledge you, dear silent (or not-so-silent) reader. If you got something out of it, great. If you want one takeaway, it would be 'pause'. And please scribble your own techniques on the sides of the page. Email them to me, and I will add them to my arsenal. If I like your techniques, I will also add them to the (hopefully) next edition of the book with citations.

Some parts of this book have appeared as essays in *Mint*, *Hindustan Times* and *The National*. Many of those have been rewritten to suit the tone of this book.

Notes

Scan this QR code to access the notes.

About the Author

Shoba Narayan is the author of six non-fiction memoirs—because one wasn't enough. As journalist and columnist, she has convinced editors at the *Hindustan Times*, *Mint Lounge*, *Condé Nast Traveler*, *Sommelier India*, *The New York Times* and other publications to publish her writings on travel, nature, culture, food and wine. She is obsessed with Indian textiles, jewellery and crafts, something that her family can confirm, based on time and money spent on these pursuits. She hosts the Bird Podcast, speaking about—and occasionally to—birds. Her children call her weird, but she prefers to think of herself as elegant-eccentric. She is the co-founder of Zapigo, a Bangalore-based tech start-up in the celebration space, because she figured that if you're going to work in tech, you might as well make it about joy. She writes poetry when stuck in Bangalore traffic and won the Erbacce Prize for Poetry 2025. Her lifelong goal is to get fit without exercising and lose weight without dieting.

Other Books by Shoba Narayan:

Monsoon Diary: A Memoir with Recipes (2004)
Return to India: An Immigrant Memoir (2012)
Katha: Tell a Story, Sell a Dream (2015)
The Milk Lady of Bangalore: An Unexpected Adventure (2019)
Food and Faith: A Pilgrim's Journey Through India (2020)
Namma Bangalore: The Soul of a Metropolis (2023)

HarperCollins *Publishers* India

At HarperCollins India, we believe in telling the best stories and finding the widest readership for our books in every format possible. We started publishing in 1992; a great deal has changed since then, but what has remained constant is the passion with which our authors write their books, the love with which readers receive them, and the sheer joy and excitement that we as publishers feel in being a part of the publishing process.

Over the years, we've had the pleasure of publishing some of the finest writing from the subcontinent and around the world, including several award-winning titles and some of the biggest bestsellers in India's publishing history. But nothing has meant more to us than the fact that millions of people have read the books we published, and that somewhere, a book of ours might have made a difference.

As we look to the future, we go back to that one word—a word which has been a driving force for us all these years.

Read.